Modern Scotland

Craig A Madden MA (Hons), PhD
Principal Teacher of History, Williamwood High School, Clarkston, Glasgow

F Norman Thompson MA (Hons), Dip Ed
Principal Teacher of History, Cathkin High School, Cambuslang

Drawings by Alexander Page

Edward Arnold

First published in Great Britain 1986 by
Edward Arnold (Publishers) Ltd, 41 Bedford Square
London WC1B 3DQ

Edward Arnold (Australia) Pty Ltd, 80 Waverley Road,
Caulfield East, Victoria 3145, Australia

British Library Cataloguing in Publication Data

Madden, Craig A.
  Modern Scotland.
  1. Scotland—Social conditions
  I. Title   II. Thompson, F. Norman
  941.1   HN398.S3

ISBN 0–7131–8417–5

Text set in 11/13 Century Schoolbook
by DP Press Limited
Printed by The Bath Press, Avon
Bound by W.H. Ware and Sons Ltd, Clevedon

Acknowledgements

The Publishers would like to thank the following for
their permission to reproduce copyright illustrations:
T & R Annan & Sons Ltd: cover & p52t &b;
BBC Hulton Picture Library: p13;
Imperial War Museum: pp17, 19t & b & 21t;
Punch Publications Ltd: p21b;
The British Library, Newspaper Library: pp26 & 27.

Contents

Preface

In a book of this size, it has not been the intention of the authors to attempt to cover all aspects of importance in Scotland today. Rather the authors have elected to concentrate on certain selected themes which are relevant to life in Scotland today, so the pupils would have the opportunity to study these themes in some depth. It was considered that this approach would maximise the interest of the pupils and facilitate the development of the various skills. As a consequence, the teacher's role is vital in expanding and developing those areas of particular interest to the pupils which are contained within the units of this book, and also, if desired, to fill in the gaps of areas of study left untouched by this book.

In almost all cases, the facing pages form a complete teaching unit, in which the basic skills of reading, writing and the development of knowledge and understanding form an integral part. Considerable importance is also given to the more advanced skills of enquiry, reconstruction and the interpretation of original sources (both written and visual), charts, diagrams and maps. It is anticipated that the text, visuals and assignments will provide the teacher with an adequate basis for constructive class discussion and activity.

In all aspects of the book the emphasis has been on variety in order to maintain and develop pupil interest in the various units. To this effect, the handling of the text, the nature of the visual content and the type of assignments all vary considerably from page to page. The pupil assignments are contained in the 'Things to Do' sections in the book, and they have been boxed for easy identification.

Unit 1

Town Life

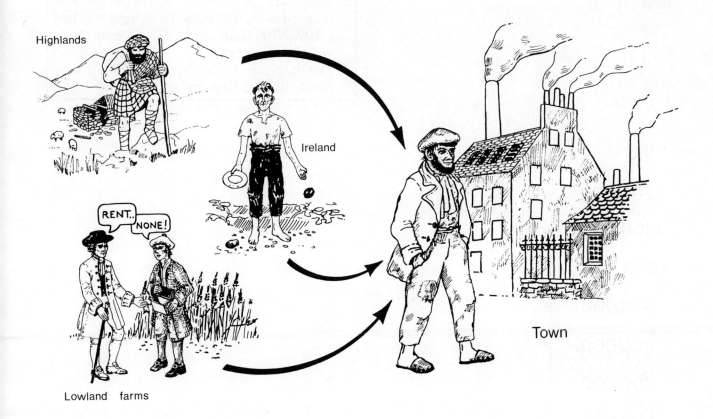

Highlands

Ireland

RENT.. NONE!

Lowland farms

Town

People Move to the Towns

About the year 1700 only a few people lived in towns. Most people lived in the countryside. They lived in cottages and worked on small farms. Their time was spent growing crops and looking after the cattle.

But between 1750 and 1850 most people left the countryside. They came in large numbers to the towns. Most of these towns were built in Central Scotland.

Why did so many people move from the countryside to the towns? The reasons are shown on the pictures above.

Things to do

1 When did people start to move to the towns?
2 The people who came to live in the towns came from ____, ____ and ____.

   Now write three sentences saying why people left each of these three places. Use the pictures to help you.
3 Write a sentence saying why people came to the towns.

Towns Grow in Size

Large numbers of people came to towns like Glasgow between 1750 and 1900. These people needed houses to live in. Land round the towns was taken over and houses were built.

Glasgow grew to be the largest town in Scotland. The number of people who live in a town is called its **population**.

Now look at the chart below. It is called a **graph**. This graph shows the number of people who lived in Glasgow between 1801 and 1981.

Things to do

1 What sort of figures are given in Line A and in Line B?
2 Make a list of the dates shown on the graph. Opposite each date write down the number of people living in Glasgow in that year.
3 Copy the graph into your workbooks. Now start at the year 1801 and join up all the dots with a line.
4 In which year was Glasgow's population at its highest?
5 Today the population of the country is counted every 10 years. This count is called a **USCNSE** (find out the word from these mixed up letters).
6 The last count was in 1981. How many people lived in Glasgow in that year?

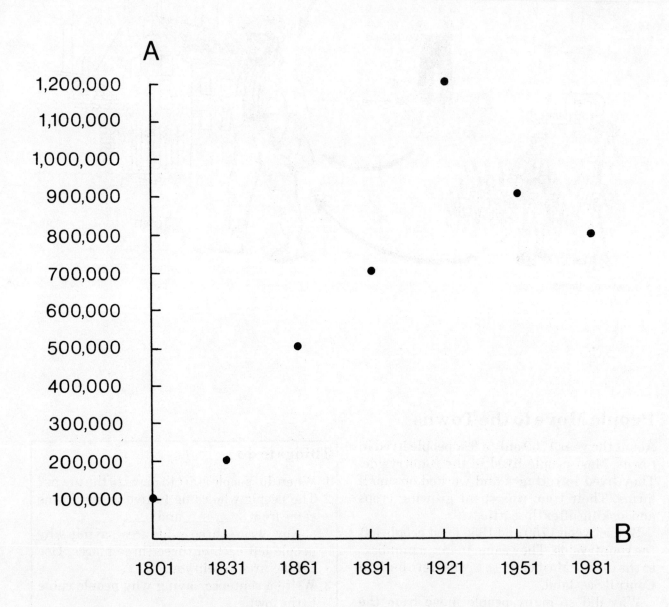

Life in the Street, 1868

By 1868 large numbers of people were working in towns. Houses were quickly built near the factories where they worked. These houses were built by the men who owned the factories. They were built close together to save money on land. As a result, the houses formed rows of dark, narrow streets. You can see such a street in the picture below.

The houses on page 7 were called **tenements**. They were often five or six floors high. Each floor was divided into single rooms. Whole families lived in each of these rooms.

Many people crowded into these tenement buildings. But the tenements had only one toilet on each floor. The rooms had no tap water. Also, there was nobody to collect the rubbish. Scraps of food and other rubbish were left in the streets. The streets were often dirty and there were rats everywhere. Both the air and houses became filthy from the smoke from the many chimneys.

These areas were called **slums**.

Things to do

Use the passage and the pictures on pages 7 and 8 to help you.

1 What was this type of house called?
2 Who built this type of house?
3 Why were the houses built so close together?
4 How many floors were there in the house at the top of the street, and also the house on the left?
5 Many of the houses were in a very poor state of repair. Can you find two clear examples of this in the picture? How would this make the houses unpleasant places in which to live?

6 Some buildings even fell down. Where does the picture show a building which has fallen down?
7 What do you notice about the surface of the street?
8 What do you think would happen to the street in heavy rain?
9 What was the only way people could dry their washing?
10 Why were there so many rats in the streets?
11 There was no tap water in the houses. Can you see from the picture where all the people in the street got their water? What problems do you think this caused?
12 The streets were often very dark. Why were they so dark (a) in daytime and (b) at night?
13 Work out how many people would live in one of these tenement houses? Make use of the figures given below.
    Each family was made up of 6 people.
    Each family had one room only.
    Each floor had 5 rooms.
    Each tenement had 5 floors.
14 How many toilets would there be in the tenement mentioned in question 13? How many people would use each of these toilets?

The picture below shows a present-day street. Write a paragraph saying how the modern street is better than that of 1868.

Donald MacDonald Comes to Glasgow

Donald MacDonald was born in the Highlands in 1855. For five years he lived in his father's farm in Glencoe. In 1860 his father was forced to leave his farm by the landlord. The MacDonald family then moved to Glasgow. There Donald's father found a job in the Springburn coal-mine.

Donald's father had very little money. He could only afford to live in a single room in a tenement in the Saltmarket. This was called a **single end**.

There is a picture of their single end on this page. It was small and cramped. But the MacDonalds were proud of it. Donald's mother always made sure that it was clean and tidy.

Why do you think it was called a **single end**?

Write a few sentences saying whether you would have liked to live in a single end, giving reasons for your decision.

Donald's Family Tree

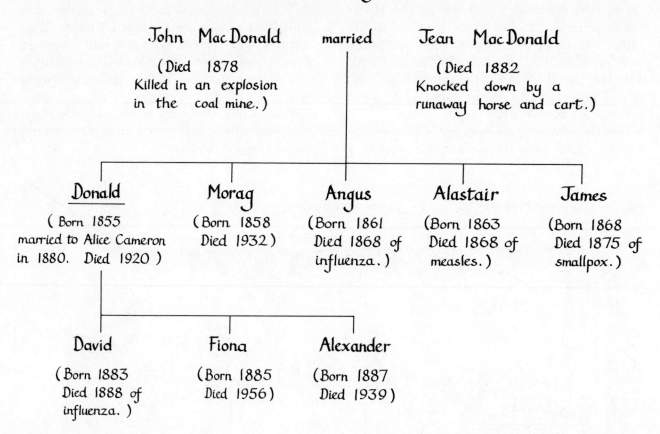

John MacDonald — married — Jean MacDonald

(Died 1878
Killed in an explosion
in the coal mine.)

(Died 1882
Knocked down by a
runaway horse and cart.)

Donald
(Born 1855
married to Alice Cameron
in 1880. Died 1920)

Morag
(Born 1858
Died 1932)

Angus
(Born 1861
Died 1868 of
influenza.)

Alastair
(Born 1863
Died 1868 of
measles.)

James
(Born 1868
Died 1875 of
smallpox.)

David
(Born 1883
Died 1888 of
influenza.)

Fiona
(Born 1885
Died 1956)

Alexander
(Born 1887
Died 1939)

Things to do

All the answers are in the family tree.
1 What are the names of Donald's father and mother?
2 How many children and grandchildren did they have altogether?
3 How many died before they reached the age of 10 years?
4 Some of those in Donald's family died as a result of a disease. Make a list of these diseases. Which of these diseases have *you* had?
5 Some died as a result of an accident of some kind. Write down an example of an accident (a) at work, (b) in the street.
6 Who in Donald's family was still alive in 1900?
7 How old was Donald when he died?

In 1900 Donald wrote a letter to his cousin Iain. Iain was still living in the Highlands. This is what Donald said in his letter.

Dear Iain,

I have spent the last 40 years living in the Saltmarket. The house there was falling to bits. The walls were damp and the ceiling has fallen in twice in the last few weeks.

I am glad to say that we have just moved into a new home. It is much better than the old one. There are two rooms and a small kitchen. We have running water and share a toilet with only one other family.

The air in our new street is much cleaner. There are no factories near us. The street is wide and gas lamps are lit at night.

I would still like to return to the Highlands. I miss the fresh air and the hills. But I hear that you have lost your job. I still work in the cotton factory. I hope to hear from you soon.

Donald

Make a list of the ways Donald's new home was better than his old one. What did Donald miss about the Highlands? In what way was Donald better off than Iain?

Glasgow Gets Bigger

We are going to see how the city of Glasgow grew in the years after 1800. Open fields and small towns were taken into the city as it increased in size.

Now look at the map below. It shows how Glasgow grew until it reached the size it is today.

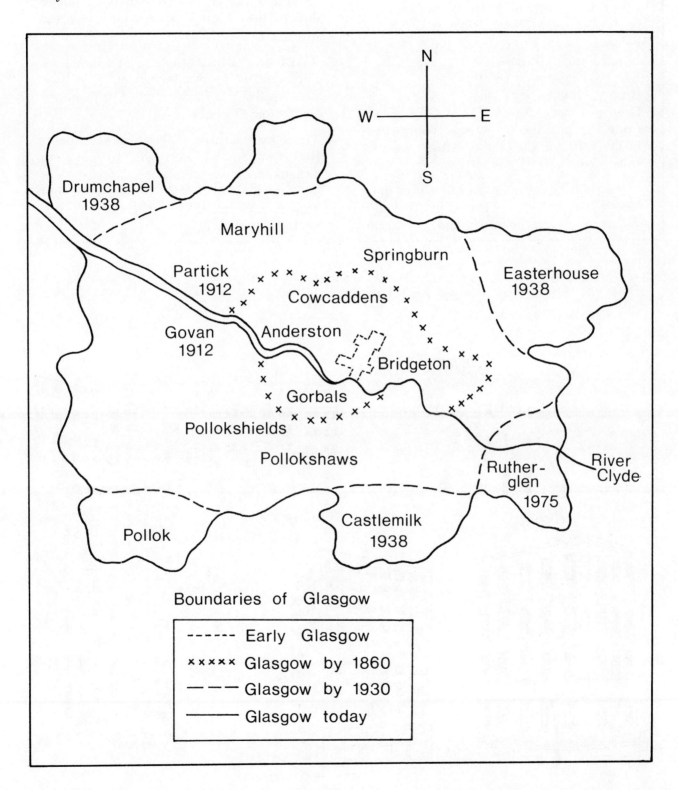

Boundaries of Glasgow

- - - - - - Early Glasgow
× × × × × Glasgow by 1860
- - - Glasgow by 1930
———— Glasgow today

Things to do

1 Draw the map on page 11 on to a piece of cardboard. It should be twice the size it is in the book. Write in the names of the different districts of Glasgow.

   The map has been divided into four parts. Each part shows the size of Glasgow at certain times. Now colour in each of the four parts of the city. Use the colour code shown below.

   Black – early Glasgow
   Red   – Glasgow by 1860
   Blue – Glasgow by 1930
   Green – Glasgow today.

2 Copy the passage below into your workbooks, filling in the blanks using the words in brackets.

   By 1860 Glasgow was growing on both sides of the River ____. It took in areas like ____ and ____ to the north, and ____ to the south. In 1912 the small towns of ____ and ____ were brought into the city. By 1938 large housing schemes in ____, ____ and ____ had grown up. In 1975 the town of ____ was taken into the city.

   In the 1960s Glasgow began to build very high flats. Some of these flats replaced older tenement houses which had been pulled down. These high flats were built in areas like ____.

   (Govan; Rutherglen; Cowcaddens; Springburn; Easterhouse; Clyde; Castlemilk; Partick; Drumchapel; Bridgeton; Gorbals)

3 These are pictures of five types of houses that would have been seen in Glasgow. Trace each house on to a piece of paper. Cut out each house. Stick the houses on to your map in an area that you would have expected to find them.

New Towns

By 1945 many of the older areas of Glasgow were not very pleasant places in which to live. Houses, factories, gasworks and railway lines were all mixed up together. It was very noisy and dirty. Such an area was Gorbals. Above is a picture of Gorbals in 1945.

In the years after 1945 many families moved away from areas like Gorbals.

Write a short paragraph saying why you would want to move away from the area in the picture.

Some of the families who moved away from Gorbals went to live in special housing areas at the edge of the city. These were called housing **schemes**. Some went to small towns away from Glasgow. Others went to the **new towns**. This movement of people was called **overspill**.

But, what is a **new town**? It is a town that is planned before it is built. Roads, shops, houses and factories are all set out in drawings and maps first. Only after that does the actual building of the new town begin.

The map shows where the new towns are in Scotland.

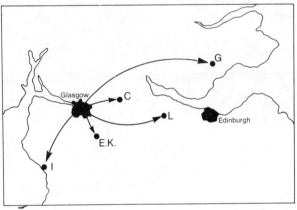

Things to do

Here is a list of the new towns.

Name and Date	Population
East Kilbride (1947)	76 000
Glenrothes (1948)	38 000
Cumbernauld (1955)	50 000
Livingston (1962)	36 000
Irvine (1966)	59 000

1 How many new towns are there in Scotland?
2 What was the first new town?
3 What is the largest new town?
4 How many people live in new towns today?

A new town was planned before it was built. The map below shows you what the land in East Kilbride was used for.

Copy the map and the key into your workbooks. Now colour in the map using this colour code:

housing – red   golf course – brown
industry – green   town centre – blue
other symbols – black

Things to do

1 Most of the land in East Kilbride is used for ____ and ____.
2 Where does the main road through East Kilbride go to?
3 What other form of transport is there?
4 What areas are set aside for sport?
5 Where do you think most of the shops are to be found?
6 How many secondary schools are there?
7 How many primary schools are there?

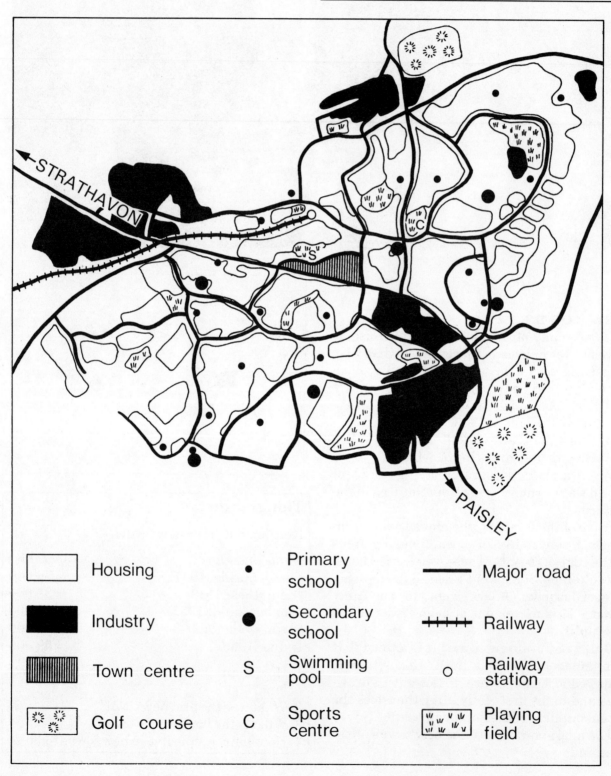

	Housing	•	Primary school	——	Major road
	Industry	●	Secondary school	+++++	Railway
	Town centre	S	Swimming pool	○	Railway station
	Golf course	C	Sports centre		Playing field

Unit 2

World War I, 1914–1918

EUROPE in 1914

D : Denmark
SE : Serbia
SW : Switzerland
G : Greece

H : Holland
R : Roumania
M : Montenegro

BE : Belgium
B : Bulgaria
A : Albania

Read this passage. It tells you about the start of a fight.

There was a big lad called **Austin**, who lived in Anytown. He had a neighbour whom people called **Seb**. Austin and Seb did not get on very well. Seb was much smaller than Austin, but he annoyed Austin. Austin wanted to teach Seb a lesson. One day he got his chance. Austin blamed Seb when somebody hit Austin's brother – Austin said Seb had helped in the attack. Austin then went looking for Seb. However, Seb had a big, strong friend called **Russell**. When Russell saw Austin hitting Seb he told Austin to stop. Austin did not stop. Instead, Austin shouted to his friend, **Gerry**, who was a good

fighter. Gerry arrived and told Russell to stay out of the fight. However, Russell decided to join in to help Seb – so Gerry joined in to help Austin.

All the noise brought other people along. Russell's friends **Fred** and **Brian** arrived. They went over to see what was happening. Gerry thought Fred and Brian had come to help Russell, so Gerry attacked Fred. Fred now joined Russell against Austin and Gerry. Brian didn't want to get involved, but just then another of Seb's friends called **Benny** came along. Gerry suddenly attacked Benny. This was too much for Brian. He now joined in.

Things to do

1 Why did Austin attack Seb in the first place?
2 Complete this sentence: Some people went to help Seb because they were his ____.
3 Copy out this sentence: When countries are friends with each other, they are called **allies**.

Put a heading: 'World War I – the two sides'.

4 (a) Beside the margin on your page, write down Austin's name. Below it write down any friends he had, taking a new line for each name.
   (b) In the middle of your page, on the same line as Austin's name, write down Seb's name. Under Seb's name make a list of all his friends, taking a new line for each name. (All the names you need are in bold type in the story).
5 (a) Put a line under the *first two letters* of each name you have written.
   (b) Now look at the map of Europe on page 15. Find the name of a country which begins with these two letters.
   (c) Write down the name of the country beside the boy's name. (<u>Au</u>stin – Au____, <u>Se</u>b –Se____).
   (d) Under the line beginning 'Austin' write down 'Britain's enemies'. Under the line beginning 'Seb' write down 'Britain's friends'.
6 Trace the map of Europe into your jotter. Shade in Britain and her friends in red; shade in Britain's enemies in blue.
7 Copy out these sentences, putting the correct word in the blank spaces.

   The First World War began in ____ and ended in ____. It went on for about ____ years. It all began when ____ attacked ____. Each country had friends or ____ who joined in to help. S____'s friends were ____, ____, ____, and ____. Their enemies were __ — and ____. These last two countries were in the (west/east/top/middle) of Europe. Because of this they were called the (Western/Eastern/Northern/Central) Powers.

More countries joined each side as the war went on. The war lasted so long, partly because most countries had been making lots of weapons for a long time. They had been doing this so they would be ready if a war did break out.

The MacGregor family lived in Rutherglen. The family was made up of the father, Jim, the mother, Jean, two sons called Peter (aged 18) and Alec (aged 20), and a daughter called Helen. Helen was 22 years old in 1914. Mr MacDonald was a postman in Rutherglen. Peter worked in a baker's shop in Main Street, and Alec worked in the butcher's shop in Mill Street. Helen had been working for three years as a maid in Castlemilk House. The family had been reading about the start of the war. They had noticed how excited many people were about fighting the Germans. Here is what the local newspaper, the *Rutherglen Reformer*, said on 7 August 1914, a Friday.

Rutherglen Territorials and the War

Wednesday night will be a memorable one. . . . Never in the history of the burgh have there been such demonstrations of enthusiasm and excitement as on the occasion of the departure of the 2nd Field Company of Engineers. The whole of Queen Street was seething with a mass of people of all ranks, men, women and children. The station entrance was blocked in such a way that the Territorials found it difficult to make their way to the train which awaited them to take them to the East Coast, where they will remain on post duty during the progress of hostilities.

A fifteen-year-old girl, telling of her experience in witnessing the departure said, 'Father it was a grand sight, and there was not a sad face in the regiment; the men were all smiling.' Yesterday there was a general look out for horses.

The Territorials will be welcomed back after peace has been regained, and that is expected very soon. At the Headquarters there are more applications for enrolment than it is possible to accept. . . . This shows the desire the youth of the country have of doing their duty.

Things to do

1 Put a heading 'The People of Rutherglen in August 1914'.
2 Answer these questions in sentences.
  (a) What was the exact date when this took place?
  (b) Why had the crowd gathered?
  (c) Where were the men to leave from?
  (d) Where were they going?
  (e) How did the crowd feel about this?
  (f) How did the soldiers feel about this?
  (g) Why do you think there was a 'general look out for horses' in 1914?
  (h) Were the soldiers expected to be away for a long time or a short time? How do you know?
  (i) Did many people want to join the army? How do you know?

What you have read was from a local newspaper. Other newspapers were read all over Scotland. Posters appeared in these newspapers to try to get people to join up. They were Recruiting Posters. One of the most popular was this one showing Lord Kitchener, the Minister of War.

3 Put a heading 'Recruiting Posters'.
4 Answer these questions in sentences.
  (a) What is a Recruiting Poster?
  (b) What do you think was the message in this poster?
  (c) Look at the picture from each side of your desk. What do you notice happening?
  (d) Why do you think the poster was made like this?

Peter and Alec MacDonald both decided they should join the army. They thought that they were needed. The same happened all over Scotland.

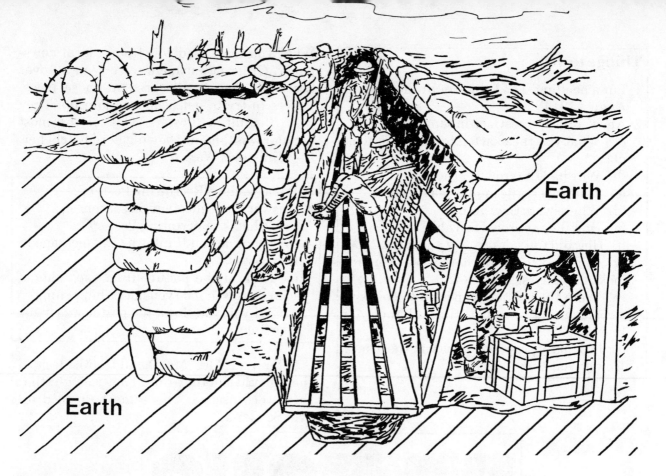

Earth

Earth

Land Fighting

The two sides in World War I could not win the war quickly, with just one battle. The enemy armies faced each other. However, if they had stayed above ground, the soldiers would have been killed. Weapons were very powerful by 1914. Both sides began to dig holes in the ground. Their soldiers stayed in these holes, so they would not be hit by enemy fire. These holes were called **trenches**. Above you can see a cross-section of a trench. This is what trenches should have been like. Quite often they were not as good as this.

A trench was 1.8 metres deep. Along the very bottom of the trench, **mud and water** would gather. The soldiers put **wooden duckboards** over this. These were pieces of wood nailed together. They could walk along the duckboards. The soldiers also built a **firestep**. They could stand on this to fire their rifles. The soldiers put **sandbags** along the front of the trench. These sandbags formed the **parapet**. The sandbags were there to stop bullets or pieces of shell hitting the soldiers. There were also **sandbags** at the back of the trench. They were there to protect the soldiers if a shell exploded behind the trench. The soldiers also made **dug-outs**. These were large holes 'dug out' of the back of the trench. The soldiers slept in these, wrote their letters, played cards and waited.

Things to do

1 In your jotter make a drawing of the cross-section of a trench.
2 Use the words in bold type in the passage to label your drawing.
3 Write a sentence saying what each of the following were used for: duck-boards; fire-step; sandbags; dug-out.
4 Look at the picture of the cross-section of the trench. Imagine that there was a great deal of rain. Write a sentence to show what would happen to the dug-out. Write another sentence to show how you think the soldiers would feel about this.

The Home Front

People who are not in the armed forces are called **civilians**. Until 1916 men only joined the British armed forces if they wanted to. However, it was quite hard for some men not to join up. Women used to come up to some of these civilians and give them a white feather. This was to tell them that they were cowards because they had not joined the armed forces. The government also ordered posters to be put up. The posters asked for men to join up or **enlist** in the armed forces. More and more men were needed because so many men were being killed in France.

Daddy, what did *YOU* do in the Great War?

Life soon began to change for many civilians, especially after January 1916. From then on, men had to join the armed forces whether they wanted to or not. This is called **conscription**.

REMEMBER THE 'LUSITANIA'

THE JURY'S VERDICT SAYS:

"We find that the said deceased died from their prolonged immersion and exhaustion in the sea eight miles south-south-west of the Old Head of Kinsale on Friday, May 7th, 1915, owing to the sinking of the R.M.S. 'Lusitania' by a torpedo fired without warning from a German submarine."

"That this appalling crime was contrary to international law and the conventions of all civilized nations, and we therefore charge the officers of the said submarine and the Emperor and Government of Germany, under whose orders they acted, with the crime of wilful and wholesale murder before the tribunal of the civilized world."

IT IS YOUR DUTY
TO TAKE UP THE SWORD OF JUSTICE
TO AVENGE THIS DEVIL'S WORK

ENLIST TO-DAY

Some people refused to join the armed forces. These people were **pacifists** who did not believe in fighting. Pacifists were known as **conscientious objectors**, or '**conshies**' for short. Some 'conshies' were put in prison. This happened to them because they did not want to take any part in the war. People thought they were cowards.

Women also faced many changes in their lives because of World War I. Even in 1914, no women were allowed to vote in general elections. Some women did not think that this was right. They demanded the right to vote. At first they tried by peaceful means to win the vote, but these failed. Later, in the years before 1914, some women had smashed windows, set fire to buildings, and one had even thrown herself in front of the King's horse at the Derby. These women were called **Suffragettes**. They had done this to draw atten-

tion to their demands. However, when the war began the women stopped these actions. Many women demanded that they should be allowed to help in the war. They could not fight, so they demanded to be allowed to work.

Things to do

1 Put a heading 'Woman in World War I'. Copy and complete these sentences.
Suffragettes were women who wanted. . . . At first, they had used peaceful methods but later, they had caused a lot of trouble; for example they had . . . (give *two* examples to complete this sentence). They had done this so that. . . . However, they stopped all this during the war because they wanted to. . . . Many women were needed to work during the war because. . . .

Propaganda

Sometimes during a war the people of a country are not told the whole truth about what is happening in the war. The government is afraid that the enemy might find out some important facts. These might help the enemy to win the war. However, a government sometimes wants to get the people to think about things in a certain way. They might want to make them hate their enemies. To do this, they might try to show that their enemies were very bad or very cruel. We call this **propaganda**.

Things to do

1 Put the heading 'Propaganda'.

2 Write a sentence to explain what you think propaganda is (use the passage above to help you). Here are two examples of propaganda. They were used in Britain.

3 Look at the first picture. Answer these questions in sentences.

(a) Who do you think the woman in the picture is supposed to be?

(b) Who are the people at the back supposed to be?

(c) Who is the person on the stretcher supposed to be?

(d) Give full details of what is happening in the picture, bringing in all the people mentioned above.

(e) What is meant by the term 'Red Cross'?

(f) Try to find out what an 'Iron Cross' was.

(g) What do you think is the message behind the poster?

(h) Trace this picture into your jotter. Put your own message below it.

4 Look at the second picture. Answer these questions in sentences.

(a) What sort of person would you expect to be dressed like the man in this picture?

(b) You often find a stand like this in a church – it often has an eagle at the top. What would you expect a person like this to be doing at this stand?

(c) Who do you think the minister is really supposed to be?

(d) Now look at the stand. What has been drawn to show that this is not one you would find in a church?

(e) Look at what the minister is saying – do you notice anything unusual about one of the words? (A dictionary might help you.)

(f) What do you think is the message behind the poster?

(g) Trace this picture into your jotter.

RED CROSS OR IRON CROSS?

WOUNDED AND A PRISONER OUR SOLDIER CRIES FOR WATER.

THE GERMAN "SISTER"

POURS IT ON THE GROUND BEFORE HIS EYES.

THERE IS NO WOMAN IN BRITAIN WHO WOULD DO IT.

THERE IS NO WOMAN IN BRITAIN WHO WILL FORGET IT.

GERMAN KAISER. "LET US PREY."

21

Rationing

The First World War was a new kind of war for British civilians. Many of them now faced danger for the first time. They also found that their lives became much less comfortable during the war.

Britain could not grow or make everything she needed. She had to bring these goods into Britain from other countries – that is, she had to **import** many goods. The Germans decided to try to stop many of these goods reaching Britain. As Britain is an island, the German leaders decided to use their submarines for this task (German submarines are called U-boats). These U-boats would sink any ships in an area called a 'war zone' round Britain.

The Germans sank many ships. (In fact the USA joined the war on Britain's side in 1917 because Germany was sinking American ships.) This meant many goods were not getting to Britain. There was a shortage of some goods. The government decided to share out what they had fairly. They began to **ration** some goods. People needed a ration card to buy these things. They were only allowed to buy a certain amount of rationed goods.

Things to do

1 Make a heading of 'The Home Front – Shortages'.
2 Use the passage above and copy out the passage below, filling in the blanks.

   Britain could not produce all she needed for herself. She had to ____ many things from other countries. The Germans decided they would try to stop this. If they could stop these goods getting to Britain, they might be able to ____ the war. The Germans used ____ for this task. They sank many ships. Because of this, ____ joined the war on Britain's side.

Dangers of Attack

British civilians also faced the danger of being killed during the First World War. German attacks took place on Britain. They came mainly from the air.

German airships and aeroplanes bombed parts of Britain. Here are the results:
(i) British casualties due to German airship raids – 1900.
(ii) British casualties due to German aeroplane raids – 2900.

---

3 Put a heading 'Civilian Casualties from Air Attack'.
4 Make a bar graph of the figures for air attack. Use a scale of 3 cm = 1000 people.

The figures used above are now divided into killed and injured.
(i) German airship raids – 500 killed; 1400 injured.
(ii) German aeroplane raids – 850 killed; 2050 injured.

---

5 Using these figures, divide your bars above into two parts, one for the number of killed and one for the number injured. Shade in the areas which show the numbers killed. Make the key to show what the shading means.
6 Make a heading 'a Zeppelin Airship'.
7 Make a sketch of the German airship shown below.
8 Answer these questions in sentences.
   (a) How long was a Zeppelin?
   (b) How fast could it fly?
   (c) How many men did it carry?
   (d) How do you think they would drop the bombs?
   (e) Can you think of why it could be dangerous to be on a Zeppelin?

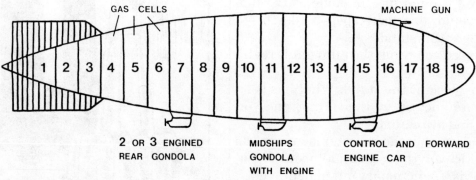

GAS CELLS   MACHINE GUN

1 2 3 4 5 6 7 8 9 10 11 12 13 14 15 16 17 18 19

2 OR 3 ENGINED REAR GONDOLA   MIDSHIPS GONDOLA WITH ENGINE   CONTROL AND FORWARD ENGINE CAR

Length : 196·5 m   Height : 27 m   Diameter : 24 m

Maximum speed : 100 kph   No. of crew : 19

Conclusion

The First World War finally came to an end in 1918. Both sides agreed to stop fighting. The fighting ended at 11.00 a.m. on 11 November 1918. This was called the **armistice**. (Many people still remember 11 November every year as Armistice Day.)

Many people had been very happy when war had begun in 1914. Men had rushed to join the armed forces. You read earlier about two brothers from Rutherglen – they soon enlisted. By 1918 they were both dead. Several million others were also dead. This made many people glad that at last the war was over – no more people would be killed. People wanted to make sure nothing like this would ever happen again. This war was sometimes called 'The War to end Wars'. Here are some of the casualty figures (excluding civilians).

Country	Killed	Wounded
Austria-Hungary	1 200 000	3 620 000
Belgium	45 000	45 000
British Empire	997 000	2 300 000
France	1 139 000	2 500 000
Germany	1 850 000	4 250 000
Italy	460 000	947 000
Russia	1 700 000	4 950 000
Serbia	50 000	134 000
USA	116 000	205 700

Things to do

1 Put a heading 'Casualty Figures'.
2 Answer these questions in sentences.
   (a) Which country had most people killed?
   (b) Which country had most people wounded?
   (c) Which country had most casualties (killed *and* wounded)? How many casualties did this country have?
   (d) How many casualties did the British Empire have?
   (e) How many casualties did Austria-Hungary have?
   (f) Think back to the two sides in the war: How many casualties did the Central Powers have? How many casualties did Britain and the countries which went to war with her in 1914 have?

Lots of property was also destroyed. The war on the Western Front was mainly fought in France and parts of Belgium. Here is some of the property lost by the French:
   1500 schools
   1200 churches
   377 public buildings
   1000 industrial plants
   246 000 other buildings
   4856 sq km of forest destroyed
   20 720 sq km of agricultural land destroyed.

3 Put a heading 'French Property Destroyed'.
4 Copy out the French losses from above.

Many ships were also lost during World War One. Here are some examples:
   Germany lost 190 428 tonnes.
   Austria-Hungary lost 15 408 tonnes.
   Britain lost 7 880 765 tonnes.
   France lost 903 003 tonnes.
   USA lost 400 972 tonnes.

5 Put a heading 'Ships Lost'.
6 Answer these questions in sentences.
   (a) Who lost most ships?
   (b) Why do you think she lost more than anybody else?
   (c) Why do you think Germany lost far less than Britain?
   (d) How many tonnes of shipping were lost by all the major powers in World War One?

However, this war did not solve the problems of the world. Most countries had many problems after the war ended. Most important, the First World War was not the 'War to end Wars'. A second World War broke out in 1939. Even more people lost their lives in this war.

7 Put a heading 'The Total Cost of the War'.
8 Try to answer this question in a sentence: Do you think all the casualties and all the other losses were worth it?

Unit 3

Scotland between the Wars

Introduction

World War I ended in November 1918. The war had lasted four years and had caused great changes in Britain. As you know, Britain introduced **conscription** in 1916. (Do you remember what conscription means?) Many more men joined the armed forces than in any war up until that time. These men had to leave their jobs to go off to fight. Many of these jobs were taken over by women, or by men who were too old to fight. These people were very important in helping to win the war.

People began to wonder what would happen to jobs now that the war had ended. The troops left the armed forces and became civilians again. This is called **demobilisation**. At first the government tried out a plan to let skilled workers leave the armed forces first. However, these men had usually joined the armed forces later than the other men. They had been kept on in the factories because their skills were needed. If they were demobilised first, this would look as if 'last in first out' was the government's aim. There were mutinies in the armed forces when this idea was tried out. The government had to change its mind. It began a scheme which meant 'first in first out'. The troops agreed with this. Most of the demobilisation was over by the summer of 1919.

At first, most of the demobilised men found jobs quite easily. During the war, people had not been able to buy many things. Factories did not make so many goods which people could use in their homes. The factories made items needed for the war effort. Now the factories began to make products which people wanted, and men were employed in the factories to make these goods. However, this only lasted about a year. Unemployment then began to rise.

There were two main reasons for this. Before World War I, Britain had mined a great deal of coal. She had also built many ships, and produced a large amount of cotton goods. Britain had sold many of these products to other countries – she had **exported** them. However, during the war, these exports had to stop. After the war, many countries did not want Britain's exports any more. Some had begun their own industries. Others received these goods from other countries. British factories had to close down.

The second reason for the unemployment was that there were very few new jobs. New factories were built, but they were often in the south-east of England. There were few new factories in Scotland, Wales and the north of England, although most of the unemployed lived there.

Unemployment began to rise in the early 1920s. Unemployment remained a problem in Britain, and especially in areas like Scotland, during the 1920s and 1930s.

Things to do

Answer these questions in sentences.

1 What does the word 'conscription' mean?
2 What happened to many of the jobs of men who had been conscripted?
3 What does the word 'demobilisation' mean?
4 Why do you think skilled men had often been conscripted later on in the war?
5 Imagine that it is the year 1919. You have been a soldier since 1914. You hear that the government is planning to demobilise skilled workers first. Write a letter to your family, telling them what you think of this plan. (Here are some words and phrases to help you: skilled workers needed at home; skilled workers last to join; fed up with the army; nice to get home again; fought for King and Country; want old job back.)
6 In your own words, explain why many of the demobilised men found it quite easy to get a job at first.
7 Why could Britain not export so many goods at the end of World War I?

Unemployment

Look at the diagram below. It is called a Bar Graph. Bar Graphs can be used to tell us about how many people were unemployed in certain years. You will notice that there is a vertical line (a line running up and down the page). In this case it shows how many people were unemployed. Then there is a horizontal line (a line running across the page). This shows a number of years. A scale is also needed for a Bar Graph. Here the scale on the vertical line is 1 cm = 400 000 people.

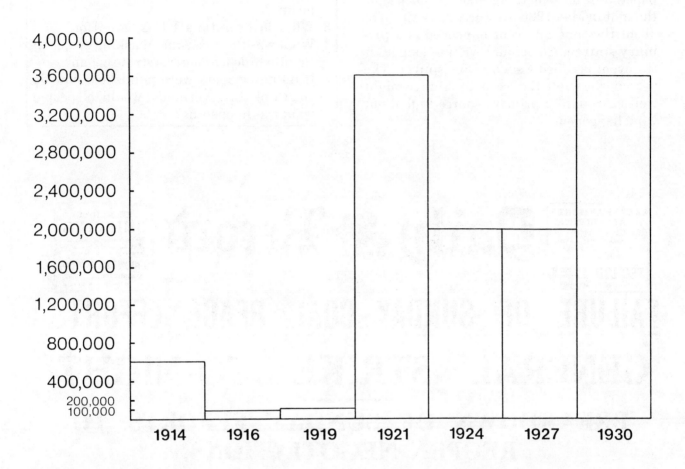

Things to do

1 This Bar Graph tells us that in 1916 there were 90 000 people out of work; in 1919 there were about 100 000 people unemployed. Use your ruler to help you find out how many people were unemployed in the other years shown here.

2 When was the biggest jump in the number of unemployed?

3 Why do you think this happened then? (Remember what you read on the last page.)

4 Why were so few people unemployed in 1916?

5 What was the biggest number of people unemployed in the 1920s?

6 Make up some Bar Graphs of your own. You could make one up with the number of people in your class whose surnames start with the letter 'A', 'B', 'C' and so on. You will need to work out a scale to fit on to your page.

The General Strike, 1926

Many important events occurred in Britain in the 1920s. They cannot all be described here. However, one of these events will be studied – the General Strike of 1926. We can learn something of the General Strike by reading newspapers printed at the time. These newspapers tell us something about what people thought in May 1926. Any account written at about the time an event happened is a **primary source**. An account written long after the event is called a **secondary source**. The person who wrote the secondary source might well have used a primary source to find out what happened.

Read this extract and answer the questions below:

Things to do
1 In which industry did the problems begin?
2 What do you think a 'General Strike' means?
3 What do the initials 'T.U.C.' stand for?
4 What was the government asking people in Britain to do if a General strike began?
5 If no newspapers were published, how do you think the government would tell people what was happening?

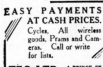  

EASY PAYMENTS AT CASH PRICES. Cycles, All wireless goods, Prams and Cameras. Call or write for lists. TEC LTD. 4 BRIDGE ST., GLASGOW, C.5 "THE FIRM TO RELY ON."

Daily ✠ Record
and Mail

ESTAB. 1847—No. 24,743.   GLASGOW, MONDAY, MAY 3, 1926.   ONE PENNY.

GENERAL SHIPPING We undertake the Shipping of all classes of Goods to or from any part of the world. UNION TRANSIT CO. 381 ARGYLE STREET, GLASGOW. Also at London and Liverpool.

FAILURE OF SUNDAY COAL PEACE EFFORTS.

GENERAL STRIKE TO-NIGHT.

BREAKDOWN OF SUNDAY EFFORTS TO REOPEN NEGOTIATIONS.

APPEAL FOR VOLUNTEERS.

*T*HE *following statement was issued from 10 Downing Street just after one this morning.* The following decision of the Government has been conveyed to Mr. Pugh, chairman of the T.U.C. Committee:—

The Government realises that no solution of the difficulties in the coal industry which is both practicable and honourable to all concerned can be reached except by sincere acceptance of the report of the Commission. In the expression "acceptance of the report" is included both reorganisation of the industry, which is to be put in hand immediately, and, pending the result of the reorganisation being attained, such interim adjustment of wages or hours of work as will make it economically possible to carry on the industry in the meantime.

If the miners or the trade unions on their behalf were prepared to say plainly they accept this proposal, the Government would have been ready to resume negotiations and to continue the subsidy for a fortnight, but since the discussions which have taken place between the miners and members of the trades union representatives, it has come to the knowledge of the Government, not only that specific instructions have been sent under the authority of the unions represented at the conference convened by the General Council of the Trade Union Congress directing their members and several of the most vital industries and services of the country to carry out a general strike on Tuesday next, but that overt acts have already taken place, including gross interference with the daily press.

Such action involves a challenge to the constitutional rights and freedom of the nation. His Majesty's Government, therefore, before it can continue negotiations, must require from the trade unions committee both a repudiation of the actions referred to that have already taken place, and an immediate and unconditional withdrawal of the instructions for a general strike.

The General Strike began on 3 May 1926. The Strike involved about 2 500 000 of the 6 000 000 trade union members in Britain. The Strike did not last very long. Only the miners remained on strike. They did not go back to work until 19 November 1926.

Below are two articles from the Glasgow Daily Record of Saturday May 15, 1926. They describe the end of the General Strike.

Things to do

1 Look at the article on the left. On which day did the General Strike 'officially' come to an end?
2 Work out the date of this day from all that you can see in this article.
3 Were the people of Scotland glad or sad that the General Strike was over? (See the article on the right.)
4 What can you see in this article which shows that things were not yet back to normal.

You can find out much more about the General Strike by looking in other books.

What you have read here tells you how some people felt about the Strike in May 1926.

We said earlier that newspapers are a primary source of evidence. We can learn more about 1926 from these two sets of items. Try to obtain a copy of a recent *Daily Record*. Look at its front page and compare it with the two shown here. Make a list of all the differences you can find (cost, presentation, etc.). Make another list of anything you notice which is the same.

Try to obtain a copy of another newspaper. See if you can spot any differences between that newspaper and a modern *Daily Record*.

SATURDAY MAY 15, 1926

RAIL SETTLEMENT.

TERMS ON WHICH MEN GO BACK TO WORK.

"NOTICE" IN FUTURE.

NO SURRENDER OF RIGHTS TO CLAIM DAMAGES.

THE railway dispute has been settled and there are hopeful signs of a coal agreement. Thus have been dispelled the depression and confusion which followed the official calling off of the General Strike on Wednesday in consequence of the almost total failure of the men to return to work on Thursday.

Railwaymen who went on strike are to be taken back as soon as work can be found for them. The unions admit that in calling the strike they committed a wrongful act, and agree that the companies do not, by reinstatement, surrender their legal rights to claim damages.

HOW SCOTLAND RECEIVED THE NEWS

It was with a feeling of genuine relief that the news of the railway settlement was received in Scotland.

To a *Daily Record* representative one railway manager said:—

"We want to see the wheels turning again; we are quite willing to let bygones be bygones, and to get on with the business of life.

"It is our intention to engage the men as the work demands it, and I am quite sure all the men will come back. They have had enough of the dispute."

In the early evening the Glasgow branches of the three railway Unions received the following telegram from headquarters:—

"Complete reinstatement secured. All members should report for duty immediately. Full details to follow."

The railway position was completely confused in the early part of yesterday as a result of the development overnight.

Certain of the staff who the day before had undertaken to return to duty did not do so. The outcome was that additional passenger trains announced for yesterday could not be run.

The settlement was reached too late to allow of arrangement for many additional passenger trains to-day. There will be an increase, however, notably about mid-day in order that business people returning to the districts may be suited.

Circumstances will not permit of either the L.M.S. or the L.N.E.R. introducing excursion facilities on Monday, the King's Birthday, so that there will be no excursion trains or fares. Trains, however, may be duplicated here and there.

The L.N.E.R. Company announce that their train services to-day will be as yesterday, with a few additions, which include the following:—

1 p.m.—Edinburgh to Glasgow.
1.15 p.m.—Glasgow to Edinburgh.
1 p.m.—Glasgow to Helensburgh; and
2.30 p.m.—Helensburgh to Glasgow.

The 3.30 p.m. train from Fort-William to Glasgow will not run to-day, and the train for Perth from Glasgow will leave at 3 p.m. instead of at 1.45 p.m.

Unemployment in the 1930s

Unemployment in Britain became much worse at the beginning of the 1930s. The figures below show the number of people unemployed:

1931	2 730 000	1936	1 700 000
1932	2 750 000	1937	1 670 000
1933	2 440 000	1938	1 800 000
1934	2 100 000	1939	1 400 000
1935	2 000 000		

Things to do

1 Make up a Bar Graph to show these figures for unemployment. Use this scale in your jotter: 1 cm = 250 000 people.

Most of these people received unemployment benefit. The pictures below show what people received each week in August 1931.

2 What did a man with a wife and two children receive?
3 What did a man with a wife and four children receive?
4 What did a widow with three children receive?
5 What did a widower with two children receive?

0·85p   0·45p   0·10p

People were expected to live on this amount of money. Even this amount was reduced later in 1931. It was meant to pay for rent, food, heating, clothes, light and everything else. Unemployment benefit would prevent a family from starving. However, they would have a very poor diet.

Things to do

1 Trace or draw the picture below into your jotter.
2 Put into the empty side some of the foods which would help to make up a balanced diet. (You may have to do some research.)

Not all unemployed people received unemployment benefit. Farm labourers, domestic servants and others who had earned more than £250 a year did not receive unemployment benefit. Most of these people had to go to the local **Poor Law Authority**. The Poor Law Authority paid out money which came from the local rates.

Soon a new problem faced the unemployed people. They could only receive unemployment benefit for 26 weeks. After this time, they would have to apply for another payment. Before this payment was made, the unemployed people had to face the **Means Test**. People asked them questions about how much savings they had, how much furniture they owned and who else in the house might be earning money. People hated the Means Test. They hated having to answer these kinds of question in front of complete strangers.

Unemployed people often received very little because of the Means Test. Sometimes they received nothing at all. One unemployed miner with a wife and six children received nothing because he had £15 saved up. He would have to use up all his savings before he could get any extra money.

---

3 Divide a page in your jotter into two columns. Write the heading *True* at the top of one column, and *False* at the top of the other. Copy out these sentences, putting them below the correct heading;
   (a) In the 1930s all unemployed people received unemployment benefit.
   (b) In the 1930s farm labourers did not receive unemployment benefit.
   (c) In the 1930s people who earned less than £250 a year received unemployment benefit.
   (d) In the 1930s people who did not receive unemployment benefit went to the Social Security Committee for help.
   (e) In the 1930s the people of Britain thought the Means Test was a good idea.
   (f) In the 1930s people had to apply for a Means Test if they had been unemployed for more than 26 weeks.
4 Imagine that you have to apply for a Means Test. Write a paragraph describing what happened. You should write down the questions you were asked; describe how you felt; and what happened at the end. Here are some words to help you: stranger came into your house; looked at every room; asked to see personal papers; upset; shame.

Unemployment and the Means Test

These pictures show what life was like for many people. They tell about unemployment and the Means Test. The pictures are not in the correct order.

Things to do

1 Write down the numbers of the pictures in the correct order.
2 Write down what each picture shows.

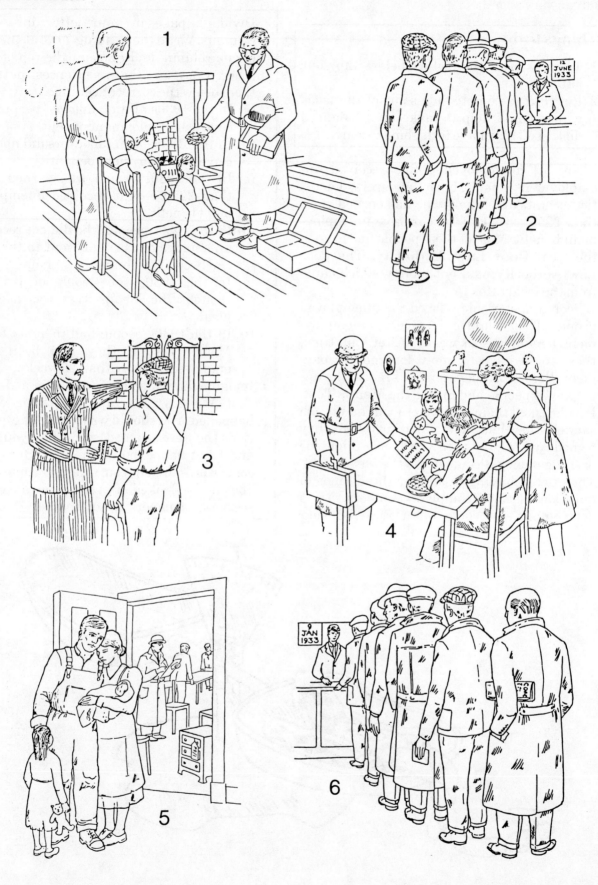

Life in the 1920s and 1930s

Not everyone was very poor in the 1920s and 1930s. Many people could buy new machines which made life easier for them. It was not until the 1920s that working people could hope to have electricity in their houses. Electricity became very popular in the 1920s and 1930s. It was supplied through cables carried on pylons. Here are some examples of articles which could be used in the home. They were all powered by electricity.

Things to do

1 Draw or trace each picture above.
2 Here are the names of each of the articles shown in the pictures. Unscramble the letters. Write the correct name under each article.

RESWISLE; UMUVAC LEANERC; NORI: CRILETEC ROOKEC; WINGASH NAMEHIC

3 Make a list of the differences between one of the articles in your picture and a modern article.

People were also able to go to the cinema for the first time. The cinema or 'Picture House' became very popular. Famous people who appeared in films were Charlie Chaplin and Buster Keaton. Walt Disney thought up the very popular Mickey Mouse. The first films were silent films. Later the 'Talkies' began. Saturday was the most popular day for going to the pictures. Many cinemas put on special shows in the afternoon. These were called **matinées**.

The wireless was also very popular. We would call a wireless set a **radio** today. The old wireless sets took several minutes to heat up. There was no sound until they heated up. They had to be tuned very carefully to find a programme. The British Broadcasting Company made all the wireless programmes. Later it was called the British Broadcasting Corporation. It still has this name today.

Using the information on this page, complete this crossword puzzle.

Clues Across:
5 An invention to help in the kitchen (7,7).
7 Sounds like new kinds of films for the cinema (7).
8 The British Broadcasting Corporation (1,1,1).
9 The first name of a famous cartoon character (6).
10 The first name of the man who thought up this famous cartoon character (4).
12 The second name of a famous filmstar (6).
13 The first name of the person in 12 Across (6).

Clues Down:
1 Probably the greatest funny man ever to appear in films (7,7).
2 A new invention in the kitchen for preparing meals (8,6).
3 You could sit at home and listen to this (8).
4 This would help to make your house spotless (6,7).
6 Good for flattening things out (4).
11 The second name of a famous cartoon character (5).

Clothes

People dressed differently in the 1920s and in the 1930s. Here are some examples of the styles of clothes which people wore.

Things to do

1 Trace these pictures into your jotter.
2 Colour in your pictures.
3 Make a list of differences you can see between clothes in the 1920s and clothes in the 1930s.
4 Write several sentences to show whether you prefer the style of the 1920s or the 1930s, or the styles of today. Give reasons for your choice.

Conclusion

You have seen how new inventions made life much easier for many people. Electric power made these possible. The cinema also made life more enjoyable for many. Sport was also very popular in the 1930s.

However, the 1920s and 1930s were terrible years for many people in Scotland in particular. As you have seen, large numbers of people were out of work. They received very little money. They were desperately poor. The hated Means Test was also introduced.

As the 1930s went on, there was a change, however. Trade began to improve. It also seemed that another war might begin. More guns were made and more ships were built, so more people were employed in factories and shipyards. In 1939, conscription was brought back again. World War II had begun.

1920's 1930's

Unit 4

World War II, 1939–1945

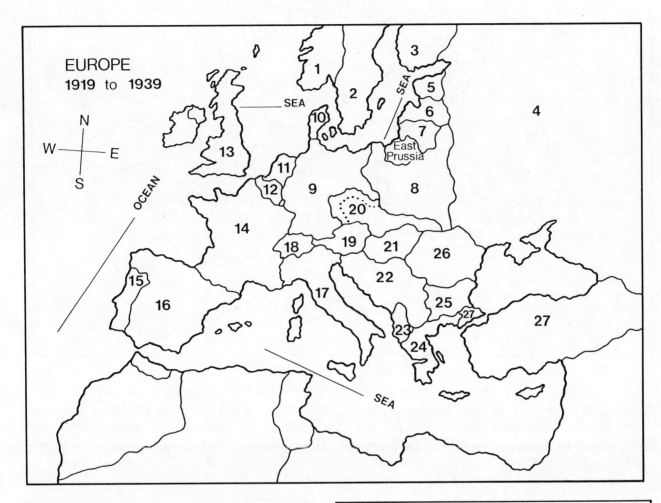

Adolf Hitler became Chancellor (Prime Minister) of Germany in 1933. He began to take over land around Germany. At first he got away with this. He took over Austria in March 1938. He took over part of Czechoslovakia in September 1938, and most of the rest of the country in March 1939. In September 1939 he attacked Poland. Britain had an agreement to help Poland if she were attacked. So Britain, and then France declared war on Germany. World War II had begun.

Things to do

1 Trace out the map 'Europe 1919 to 1939'.
2 Make a list of the numbers 1 to 27 down the side of your map.
3 Using an atlas, put in the name of each country beside the number you have written at the side of your map.
4 Put in the names of the seas and the oceans on your map.
5 Shade in Germany with a black pencil (including East Prussia which belonged to Germany).
6 Shade in Austria with a brown pencil.
7 Shade in the border between Czechoslovakia and Germany with a green pencil. There is a dotted line on the map for this.
8 Shade in the rest of Czechoslovakia with a blue pencil.
9 Shade in the western half of Poland with a yellow pencil.
10 Make a key: Add a box with each of the colours brown, green, blue and yellow. Beside each box, put the name of the country, and when it was taken over.
11 Shade in Italy with a black pencil.
12 Make another key: Put in a box with black shading. Beside it, write 'Germany and Italy, the Enemies of Britain'.

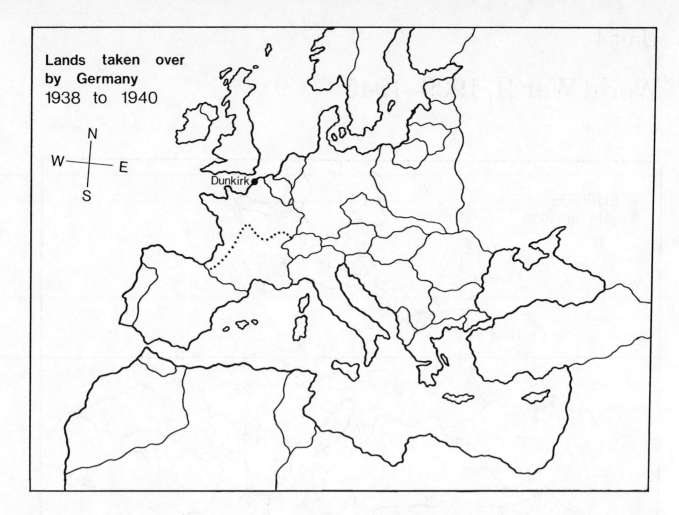

Lands taken over by Germany 1938 to 1940

N W E S

Dunkirk

The war began in 1939. However, at first Britain was involved in very little fighting. Some raids by aircraft took place. Then in April 1940 Germany suddenly took over Denmark, and attacked and took over Norway.

diers. Then the boats went back over to France to collect more soldiers. The Germans attacked the soldiers and the boats all the time. These boats brought back over 300 000 soldiers to Britain. The Germans went on to take over a large part of France.

Things to do

1 Trace the map 'Lands Taken over by Germany, 1938 to 1940' into your jotter.
2 Colour in all the countries Germany had taken over before 1940 in black (your map of 'Europe 1919 to 1939' should help you). Make a key to show what the black colour means.
3 Now shade in the countries Germany attacked in April 1940, in red. Make a key to show what the red colour means.

However, the Germans did not stop there. On 10 May 1940, Germany attacked France. British troops had gone to help the French. They were driven back to the port of Dunkirk. The soldiers waited on the beaches to be rescued. Over 850 small boats were collected in Britain. They were sailed over to France. They helped to bring back many of the sol-

4 On your map, shade in the north and west of France, down to the dotted line. Use a blue pencil. Shade in Belgium, the Netherlands and Luxembourg in blue. Make a key to show that this was land taken by Germany in May 1940.

Germany and the USSR had an agreement not to fight each other. They had made this agreement in August 1939. This meant that the USSR was a friend or **ally** of Germany. Then in June 1940, Italy decided to join Germany. Before this, Germany and Italy had helped a new Spanish leader to take power. Hitler now hoped that Spain would help him.

5 Using a green pencil, draw diagonal lines across Italy, Spain and the USSR. Make a key to show that they were allies or friends of Germany.

Bombing

When war began, ordinary people in Britain expected they would be attacked. They thought they would be attacked from the air by gas bombs and high explosive bombs. But although high explosive bombs were used, no gas bombs were dropped.

Gas

People were very afraid of gas. They were afraid because nobody could see the gas. This was what made it so dangerous. Even before the war began, people were given gas masks. There were different kinds of gas mask. Children were given masks which were sometimes made of red rubber. They were meant to look like Mickey Mouse. The idea was to make the children want to wear them. Gas masks had to fit very tightly. Special gas masks were used for babies. The babies were very frightened when they had to be put on. Below are three pictures of gas masks.

Things to do

1 Make a drawing or tracing of one of the adult gas masks. Label your picture. Below it, write down what each part would be used for.
2 Why do you think that most people did not like to wear them very much?
3 Make a sketch of the gas mask for babies.
4 What do you think the 'left arm' would be used for?
5 Do you think these would be easy to put on to the babies? Give reasons.

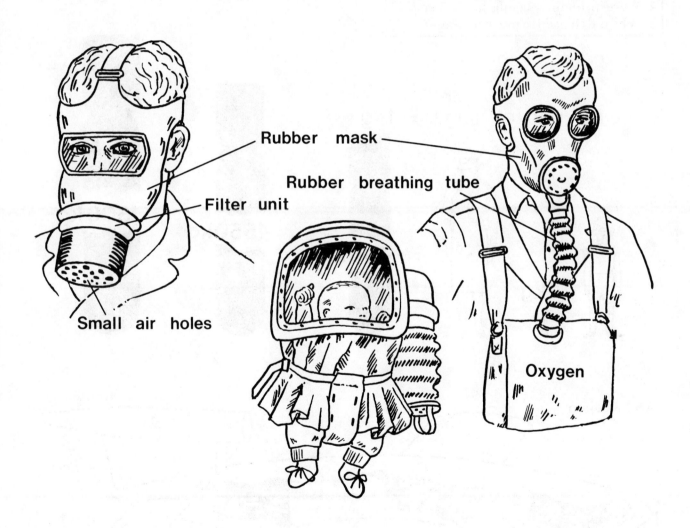

Rubber mask

Rubber breathing tube

Filter unit

Small air holes

Oxygen

High Explosive Bombs

Many high explosive bombs were dropped on Britain. The time when these bombs were dropped is called the 'Blitz'. There were many different kinds of bomb.

The big bombs were very powerful. They could destroy buildings and blow people into tiny pieces. The small bombs were also very dangerous. Some of them were called **incendiary bombs**. This meant that they were fire bombs. Lots of these were dropped together. They could start terrible fires.

Later Bombing

Later in the war, the Germans made 'Flying Bombs'. A 'Flying Bomb' was also known as a 'V1'. They had no pilots. They just flew on until they ran out of fuel. People could hear their engines. When the engine stopped, they had to run for shelter. The Germans used about 8000 V1 bombs. Then they began to use Rockets. They were called 'V2' weapons. They travelled very quickly. People could not hear them coming. About 1000 of these reached Britain.

Things to do

1 Put a heading 'Bombing' in your jotter.
2 Look at the picture of the bombs. How many bags of sugar could you put into an 1800 kg bomb?
3 What was an incendiary bomb?
4 Were incendiary bombs large or small?
5 Why did they do so much damage?

---

6 Make a sketch of the V1 weapon.
7 What kind of weapon was a V2?
8 Do you think people would be more afraid of a V1 weapon or a V2 weapon? Give reasons.

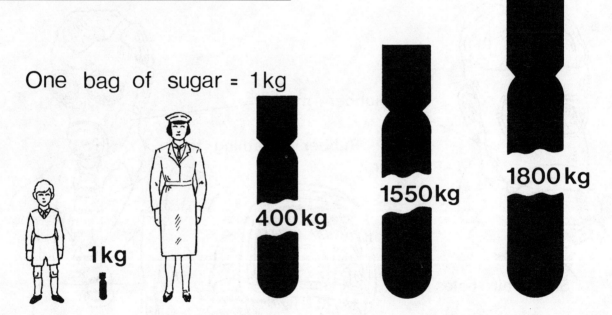

One bag of sugar = 1kg

1kg   400kg   1550kg   1800kg

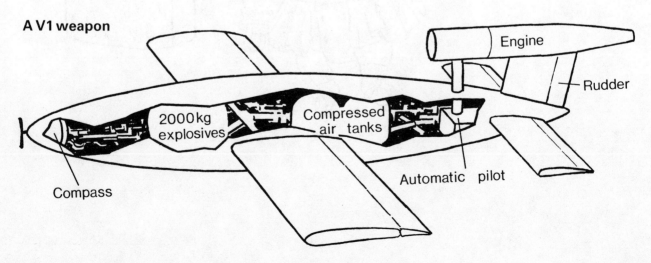

A V1 weapon

Engine

Rudder

2000kg explosives

Compressed air tanks

Automatic pilot

Compass

Shelters

Everyone expected the Germans to bomb Britain. It was important that people could be safe from bombs. Shelters were given out to many families. There were different kinds of shelter. Here are two examples:

The Anderson Shelter

Look at the picture of an Anderson Shelter. It would keep people safe, unless there was a direct hit from a bomb.

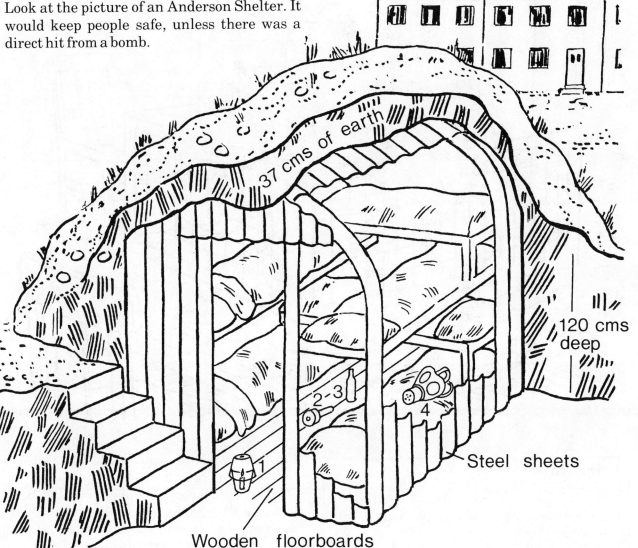

37 cms of earth

120 cms deep

Steel sheets

2-3

4

1

Wooden floorboards

Things to do

1 Put a heading 'The Anderson Shelter' in your jotter. Answer these questions in sentences:

(a) If you were going to build an Anderson Shelter, what would be the first thing you would have had to do?

(b) How much earth would have to be put on top?

(c) Where would the earth come from?

(d) Why would this have to be done?

(e) How many people could an Anderson Shelter sleep?

(f) Look for the numbers 1 to 4 in the drawing. Write these numbers into your jotter. Beside each number, write down what each number is showing. Then write down why you think people might need each of these things.

(g) Do you think that it would have been comfortable or uncomfortable in an Anderson Shelter? Give reasons for your answer.

(h) What kind of home would you have had to live in if you were to use an Anderson Shelter?

The Morrison Shelter

Look at the picture of a Morrison Shelter.

Things to do

1 Put a heading 'The Morrison Shelter' in your jotter. Answer these questions in sentences:

(a) In what kind of homes would the Morrison Shelters be useful?

(b) What sort of people would find the Morrison Shelters useful?

(c) What else could the Shelter be used for?

(d) How would you get into the Shelter?

(e) In what ways would the Morrison Shelter be better than the Anderson Shelter?

(f) Can you think of any dangers in using a Morrison Shelter?

People in London suffered very badly because of German bombing. Many of them used another kind of shelter. At night, they used the London Underground stations. People in other towns also suffered. In Scotland, the town of Clydebank was attacked by German bombers in March 1941. The people of Clydebank had very poor shelters. Clydebank had about 12 000 houses. Only seven of them were not damaged in these German attacks. There were 47 000 people living in Clydebank. The raids made 35 000 people homeless.

Many children were sent out of the towns and cities to the country. They were sent there to be safe, in case bombs were dropped on their homes. This move to the country was called **evacuation**. Children were evacuated from Glasgow. Many of them were sent to the country quite near Aberdeen.

Many of the children were very unhappy. However, others liked the countryside. Some had never been in the country before. They did not even know what some of the farm animals were called. They found that living in the country was very different from living in a town.

Rationing

ON HIS MAJESTY'S SERVICE

OFFICIAL PAID

Consumer's Name } ....

Address ....

....

....

Date of Issue
....
IF FOUND RETURN TO
....
FOOD OFFICE

Serial Number
of Book
SP 100252

SUGAR	SUGAR	SUGAR	SUGAR	SUGAR
23	19	13	7	1
24	20	14	8	2
Child's Name		15	9	3
Address		SUGAR 16	SUGAR 10	SUGAR 4
Parent's or Guardian's Signature				
26	21	17	11	5
25	22	18	12	6

PAGE 5 SUGAR COUNTERFOIL
Child's Name ....
Address ....
Date ....
Name and Address ....
of Retailer ....

SP 100252

MEAT	MEAT	MEAT	MEAT	MEAT
24	21	18	15	11
24	21	18	15	11
				12
PAGE 2				12
Consumer's Name				12
Address				12
....				
26	22	19	16	13
26	22	19	16	13
26	22	19	16	13
25	23	20	17	14
25	23	20	17	14
25	23	20	17	14

Think of the answers to these questions about your own lives today:

Who usually does the shopping in your home?

When someone goes to buy the food today, what sort of things do they usually have to think about?

People today usually have a choice of food when they go shopping. There is usually plenty of food in Britain. The shelves in our supermarkets are full of food. However, in World War II, some foods were in very short supply. The food had to be shared out fairly. The government began **rationing** to try to make sure that everyone had a fair share of certain kinds of food. Ration books were printed. There are some pages from a ration book at the top of the page.

People still had to pay for their food. However, they could only buy certain foods if they had the right coupons in their ration book. The number of coupons they were given for these foods depended on the size of the family. This was a fair system, since everyone was treated the same.

Things to do

1 Make a heading 'Food Rationing' and answer these questions in sentences.
   (a) What was rationing?
   (b) Why was it begun?
2 Look at the pages of the ration book and make a copy of them. Fill in your own name and address, as if this were your own ration book.

The amount of food which people could have was changed. Here is an example of how much an adult could have each week of some foods: one egg; sixty gm of tea; nine pence worth of meat; one thousand, one hundred and eighty five gm of milk; one hundred and fifteen gm of ham; thirty gm of cheese; two hundred and twenty five gm of fat (including butter); two hundred and twenty five gm of sugar.

3 Below are a number of drawings. Copy them into your jotter.
4 Opposite each one, write in how much an adult was allowed to have each week. Put the amount down in **figures**.

	Male		Female	
	Child	*Adult*	*Child*	*Adult*
Hat	–	–	–	–
Coat	11	16	11	14
Gloves	2	2	2	2
Scarf	2	2	2	2
Pullover (Cardigan)	3	5	3	5
Shoes	3	7	3	5
Long Trousers (Dress)	6	8	8	11
Socks	1	3	1	1

Cloth became scarce so it could not be wasted. One example of this was that no turn-ups were to be made on trousers. It also became very hard to obtain some items of clothing, for example, ladies' stockings. There is a story of one woman who dyed her legs with onion skins to make it look as if she was wearing stockings. Old material was made into clothing. Clothes were also rationed.

Above is a table showing how many coupons were needed for certain clothes:

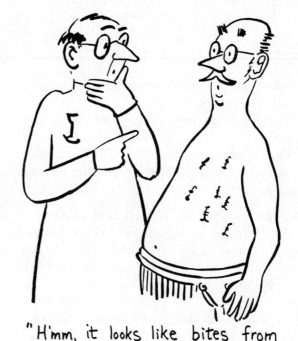

"H'mm, it looks like bites from a squander bug."

Things to do

1 Make a heading 'Clothes Rationing' in your jotter.
   (a) Make a list of items for which the number of coupons is the same for boys and girls.
   (b) Make a list of items where the number of coupons is different for boys and girls.
   (c) Make a list of items where the number of coupons is the same for men as for women.
   (d) Make a list of items where the number of coupons is different for men and women.
   (e) Why do you think there were differences in the number of coupons men and women needed for some items?

During the war, the government put up posters. Some of these posters were meant to stop people wasting food or materials. The cartoon is an example.

2 Make a heading 'Posters against Waste' in your jotter.
3 Look at the picture above. Answer these questions in sentences.
   (a) Who do you think the man on the left is supposed to be?
   (b) What do you think a 'Squander Bug' is supposed to be?
   (c) The man on the right has been bitten by the Squander Bug – write down *two* pieces of evidence from the picture to show this.
4 Make up your own little figure which could be used in a poster against waste.
5 Make up a poster using your own figure.

The Invasion of Europe

On 6 June 1944, the Allies began their invasion of France which was occupied by the Germans. This was known as 'Operation Overlord' or 'D-Day'. The Allies invaded from Britain. They started to push the Germans back. However, the war went on for nearly another year before the Germans surrendered. Here are lists of the casualty figures for the allies round about the time when they landed in Normandy in France.

From 6 June until 22 June:

	Britain	USA
Killed	2 006	3 012
Wounded	8 776	15 362

From 23 June until 20 July:

	Britain	USA
Killed	3 894	6 898
Wounded	18 314	32 443

From 11 July until 19 July:

	Britain	USA
Killed	6 010	10 641
Wounded	28 690	51 387

Things to do

1 Make a heading 'Allied Casualties in Normandy, 1944'.

2 Answer these questions in sentences.

(a) When were most American men wounded?

(b) When were most American men killed?

(c) When were most British men wounded?

(d) When were most British men killed?

(e) What do you notice happening to the numbers of killed and wounded as time went on?

(f) What was the total number of American soldiers (i) killed; and (ii) wounded?

(g) What was the total number of British soldiers (i) killed; and (ii) wounded?

(h) How many more American soldiers were killed than British soldiers?

(i) How many more American soldiers were wounded than British soldiers?

Casualty Figures

It is hard to obtain the figures for the number of people killed from some countries. Opposite are the best figures available for the dead of some countries in World War II. The scale used in the graph is 1cm = 1 000 000 people.

3 Using your ruler, work out the number killed in each of the countries below.

4 How many people were killed altogether?

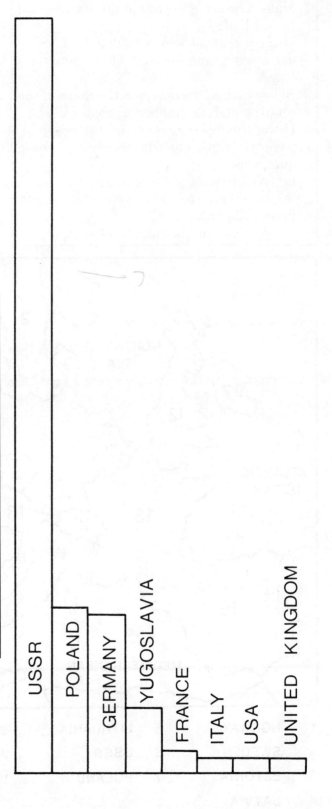

Below are the numbers of people killed in five other countries:

Czechoslovakia	– 370 000
Austria	– 340 000
Netherlands	– 200 000
Belgium	– 90 000
Norway	– 10 000

Things to do

1 Make a heading in your jotter 'Numbers of People Killed'.
2 Using a scale of 1cm = 20 000 dead, make out a bar graph for each of the countries listed.
3 Below each of the bars, put the name of the country, and the number of people killed.
4 Using the figures above and the graph on page 41, work out the answers to these questions.
   (a) Which country lost most people?
   (b) How do you feel when you read casualty figures like these?
   (c) Why do you think you feel like this?

Conclusion

In Europe, the Second World War came to an end in May 1945. Hitler committed suicide on 30 April 1945. On 7 May, a group of German army leaders offered the German surrender. This was accepted by the Allies on 8 May. This date is sometimes called 'V-E Day'. (Can you work out why it might be called this?) The war against Japan continued for several more months. The Americans dropped two atomic bombs on Japan. The Japanese surrender was accepted by the Allies on 14 August, 1945. The surrender was signed on 2 September.

Europe After 1945

The map on page 43 gives the names of the countries of Europe after 1945. The numbers on both maps below stand for the same countries.

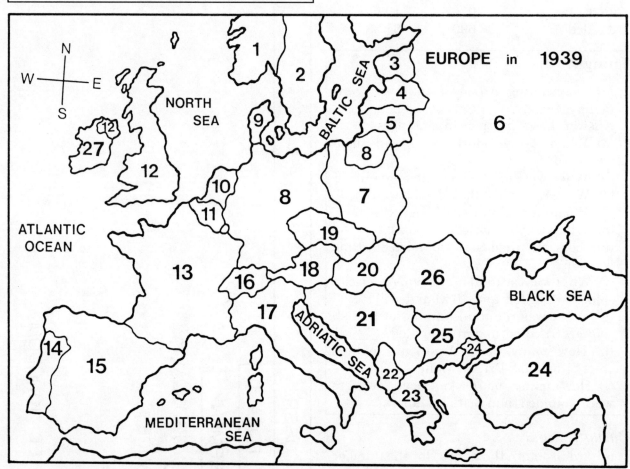

1	NORWAY	5	LITHUANIA	8	GERMANY	11	BELGIUM
2	SWEDEN	6	USSR	9	DENMARK	12	U.K.
3	ESTONIA	7	POLAND	10	HOLLAND	13	FRANCE
4	LATVIA						

Things to do

1 Put a heading 'Changes in the Map of Europe'.
2 Make a list of the countries which changed in shape from 1939 to 1945.
3 Which country gained most land from 1939 to 1945?
4 What has happened to Germany?
5 Trace the map below into your jotter. Above it put the heading 'Europe after World War II'.

6 Look at the map which you traced into your jotter.
7 Shade in all the Communist countries in Europe with a red pencil.
8 Make a key to show what the red colour means.
9 In a sentence, explain where the Communist countries of Europe are to be found.
10 Why do you think this is where they are to be found?
11 In which part of Europe are the non-Communist countries to be found?
12 There is a special name which is sometimes given to the boundary between the Communist countries and the non-Communist countries. Try to find out what it is called. Then draw this 'boundary' on to your map.

In 1945, and the next few years, a number of countries in Europe became Communist. These countries were Poland, Estonia, Czechoslovakia, Lithuania, Hungary, Rumania, Latvia, Bulgaria, Yugoslavia, Albania and East Germany. The USSR was already a Communist country.

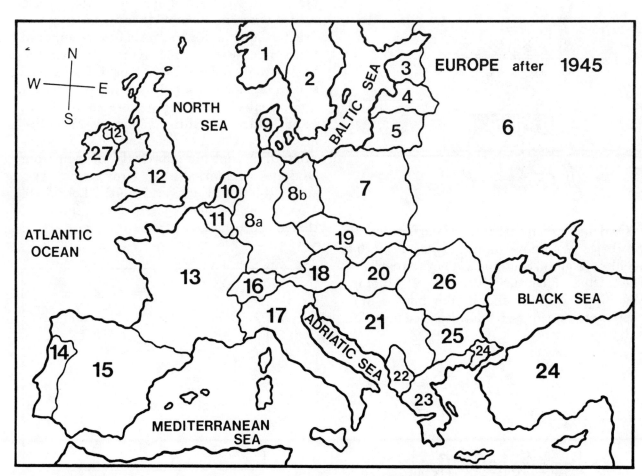

14	PORTUGAL	18	AUSTRIA	21	YUGOSLAVIA	24	TURKEY
15	SPAIN	19	CZECHO-	22	ALBANIA	25	BULGARIA
16	SWITZERLAND		SLOVAKIA	23	GREECE	26	RUMANIA
17	ITALY	20	HUNGARY			27	EIRE

43

Unit 5

Industry

Coal-Mining

In Book Two you will have read about how the Industrial Revolution began. Factories were built and machines were used for the first time. The first industry to grow up in Scotland was the cloth industry, or the textile industry. At first water power was used for the machines. There were problems with using water to power machines. Perhaps you could think of one problem which might occur in the summer, and one problem which might occur in winter.

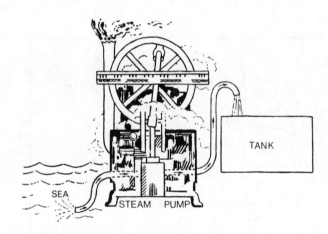

Coal had been mined in Scotland for several centuries. We know that coal was cut by the monks of some of Scotland's abbeys as early as the thirteenth century. It was used as fuel in the king's castles, and in the houses and castles of some lords. It was also used to make salt from sea water.

Things to do

1 Draw or trace the diagrams.
2 Below your pictures, explain how salt was made.

The invention of the steam-engine was very important to the coal industry. Steam power could be used to pump water out of coal-mines, and bring up coal. This meant mines could go deeper underground. New coalfields could be opened.

New inventions and new discoveries meant more coal was needed. The invention of the railway engine meant there was a much greater demand for coal. About one hundred years ago, the United Kingdom was the largest coal producer in the world. There were several Scottish coalfields which produced a great deal of coal. There were coalfields in Lanarkshire, Ayrshire, Fife and the Lothians. A great deal of Scotland's coal was **exported**, or sent abroad. Coal was sent from Glasgow (Lanarkshire), Ardrossan (Ayrshire), Methil (Fife), and Leith (Lothians). Most ships also used coal at the beginning of this century.

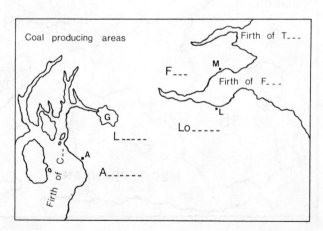

3 Trace this map into your jotter.
4 Use an atlas and the passage above to complete the place names.

In the twentieth century, working conditions in the coal-mines have improved. You can see from the pictures below what working conditions were like for men, women and children early in the last century.

Conditions are much better than this in coal-mines today. Much more machinery is used. However, it is still very hard work. It can also be very dangerous. Now machines are used to cut coal. They have large spikes, and they dig into the coal face. You can see an example of this below.

Special conveyor belts carry the coal away. You can see an example in the picture below.

Coal can be moved by using diesel locomotives.

Things to do

1 Draw or trace the pictures above.
2 Below each picture, write down what it shows.
3 Imagine you are one of these people. Try to explain what you feel about your work.

4 Draw or trace each picture above.
5 Write below each picture why it makes work much easier for modern miners.

Up until 1947, coal-mines were owned by families or by firms. In 1947, most of the mines were **nationalised**, which means they were taken over to be run by the state. The National Coal Board was set up to run the coal industry. There have been many changes since then. Many mines have been closed. This has often led to high unemployment in some parts of Scotland. New forms of energy have developed. North Sea oil has become important. Nuclear power stations are also used.

In the early years of the twentieth century, the mine-owners allowed the waste from the mines to be dumped. They formed coal 'bings'. More recently, there have been attempts to make these look more attractive. Sometimes they have been dug out and removed. Sometimes grass or trees have been planted on them. This has been done to try to improve our **environment** (the countryside around us).

You should be able to learn a lot about the mining industry by visiting parts of East Lothian. You can see mining exhibits at Prestongrange, at Prestonpans, with its famous Beam Engine. You can also visit the Lady Victoria colliery, near Newtongrange. A number of Scotland's coal-mines are in danger of being closed. The map below shows some of Scotland's pits in 1983. Here is a list of the names of some of the pits: Solsgirth, Bilston Glen, Barony, Polkemmet, Polmaise, Monktonhall, Cardowan, Francis, Comrie, Seafield, Bogside, Killoch.

Things to do
1 Trace the map into your jotter.
2 Using the list, write in the name of each pit.

Iron and steel

Coal was also very important in the development of the iron and steel industries and for shipbuilding. Iron is obtained from iron ore which was found in Scotland. The iron ore has to be heated to a great temperature. The first main ironworks in Scotland, the Carron Iron works, were built near Falkirk. Later ironworks were built in parts of the north of Ayrshire and around Motherwell, Coatbridge and Glasgow. Iron was used for a whole variety of goods. It was used in people's homes for things such as stoves, in industry for machines, and also to make ships.

Steel is another form of iron, but it is stronger than iron. Steel began to be used more and more in place of iron. This began to happen in the last century, and has gone on into this century. Scotland had a number of important iron and steel works. You can see from the map opposite where some of these were to be found. However, now there really only remains the Ravenscraig Works in Motherwell. Ravenscraig carries out all the processes from the iron-ore stage right up to finished steel.

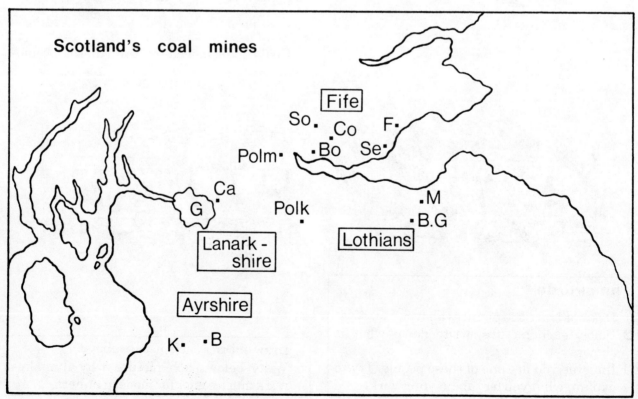

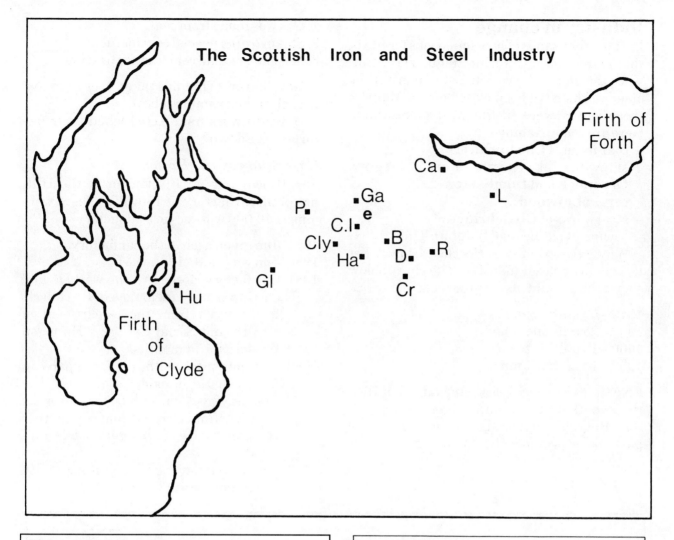

The Scottish Iron and Steel Industry

Firth of Forth

Ca.

Firth of Clyde

Ga
P.
e
C.I.
Cly.
Ha.
Hu
Gl
B
D.
R
Cr
L

Things to do

1 Trace the map above into your jotter.
2 Put the correct name beside each place on the map, using this list of names to help you: Livingston, Dalziel, Hunterston, Parkhead, Craigneuk, Gartcosh, Bellshill, Carron, Ravenscraig, Clydebridge, Hallside, Clyde Iron, Glengarnock.
3 Try to find out which of these are no longer working. Lightly score out these placenames on your map.

Shipbuilding

Ships have been built for a long time in Scotland. Clydeside became the most important shipbuilding area in Scotland. Clydeside had supplies of steel from the steelworks which were not too far away. By the beginning of this century, Clydeside was the leading shipbuilding area in the world. However, there have been great changes here, too. The map on the right shows how the shipyards were reorganised on the Clyde. The map also shows the other main shipbuilding firms in Scotland.

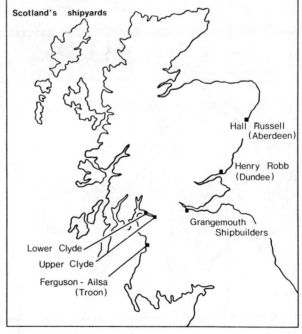

Scotland's shipyards

Hall Russell (Aberdeen)

Henry Robb (Dundee)

Grangemouth Shipbuilders

Lower Clyde
Upper Clyde
Ferguson - Ailsa (Troon)

47

Industry in change

In 1900, thousands of men found jobs for life in the many manufacturing industries. But, since the end of the war in 1945, many of the older works have been closed down. Many of these works were in the west of Scotland. Here are some examples:
– coal-mine at **Cardowan** (1)
– shipyards at **Govan**, **Port Glasgow**, **Greenock** and **Dumbarton** (2)
– cars at **Linwood** (3)
– steel works at **Clydebridge** (4)
– sewing machines at **Clydebank** (5)

Why have so many works closed down? Let us look at the coal industry. The chart below shows the amount of coal produced:

1910 – 50 million tonnes
1930 – 25 million tonnes
1960 – 18 million tonnes
1980 – 10 million tonnes

Five times more coal was being mined in 1910 than in 1980. Some mines have run out of coal. But coal is not used so much today. In the past, coal was used for the following:

1. *Gas* was made from coal.
2. Steam *trains* needed coal for fuel.
3. Most *houses* had coal fires for heating.

Now find out what has taken over from coal in each of the examples above.

How are workers affected when their factories close down?

Case Study of Jim Brown

Jim Brown was an Electrician at the Hillman Imp car factory at Linwood. There were almost 10 000 workers in that factory.

1971 Jim given a job in the car factory.
1980 Jim was paid £120 a week.
1981 Car factory closed. All the workers laid off. Jim is now unemployed. He collects £26 a week from the Department of Health and Social Security. He is 'on the dole' for 14 months.
1982 Jim gets a job with a TV company in Linwood. He is paid £80 a week. The company goes out of business after six months. Jim is 'on the dole' for another six months. He cannot get a job in Linwood.
1983 Jim leaves Linwood. He gets a job with an oil company in Orkney.

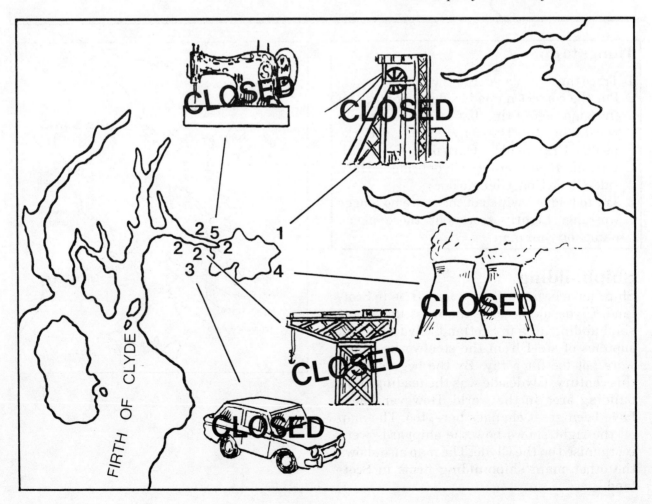

New Industries

As older industries close down, new ones are opening up in Scotland. Over 200 new factories have started in the **electronics** industry. These factories, like IBM in Greenock, Motorola in East Kilbride and Nippon Electric in Livingston, employ almost 40 000 people. Much of the work in this industry is done by machines, such as robots and computers. This is called **automation**. Also, many of these electrical products are made very small indeed. This has been possible with the invention of the **microchip**. This is a tiny 8mm square chip of **silicon**.

Other important industries are **oil** and **gas**. Large amounts of both oil and gas have been found below the sea-bed in the North Sea. Large oil companies are based in Aberdeen and Glasgow. The oil rigs are supplied from the east coast ports of Aberdeen, Peterhead, Montrose and Lerwick.

Look at the pictures below. Make a list of the things made in the **electronics** industry. Make a list of the things made from **oil**.

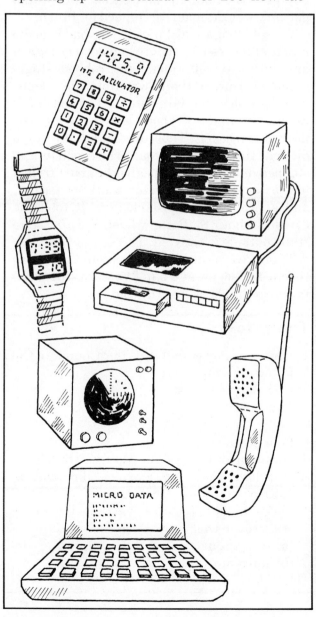

49

Unit 6

Transport

Travel in 1700

Today there are many ways to travel long distances. You can go by boat, car, bus, train or plane.

But, in 1700 most people had to walk if they wanted to go anywhere. As a result, poorer people seldom went far from their homes.

Farmers had some money and were able to travel by horse. Rich people could afford to travel by stage-coach. Heavy or bulky goods went from place to place by cart or packhorse.

However, most of the roads in 1700 were little better than tracks. There are two pictures of them below.

In 1758 Lady Jane Stewart travelled from Edinburgh to Glasgow. Here is her story:

Winter

Summer

'The stagecoach left Edinburgh at 7 a.m. I went inside the coach with another seven passengers. It was very cramped with little room for your legs. Also the dust from the horses came straight in the open windows. Ruts and holes in the road made it very bumpy. Each big bump sent us falling on top of each other.

It was cheap to travel on top of the coach. But it was very dangerous. Some passengers actually fell off if the coach went over large bumps in the road. In bad weather they would get very wet. At noon we stopped for lunch.

We set off again at 1 p.m. There had been no real problems so far. There had been no sign of any highwaymen [men who robbed stage-coaches]. But, without warning, one of our wheels broke on a large stone. The coach fell to one side and everybody was thrown to the floor of the coach. Those on top fell off into a ditch at the side of the road. The coach finally stopped on its side. I was alright apart from a few bruises. But, one person was knocked out, and another had a broken arm. It took the driver an hour to fix the wheel. We all had to stand outside in the cold.

There were no other problems, and we reached Glasgow at 8 p.m. We were still shaking with the shock and the cold.'

Things to do

1 How did they travel in 1700? Complete the following sentences:
  Rich people . . . .
  Farmers . . . .
  Coal . . . .
  Poor people . . . .
2 How long did Lady Jane's journey take?
3 How long would that journey take today by train or car?
4 Make a list of the ways that travel by stagecoach was:
  (a) dangerous
  (b) uncomfortable
  (c) slow.

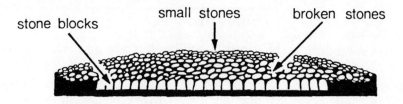

"Thomas Telford's New Road"

stone blocks   small stones   broken stones

IRON

COAL

Forth & Clyde Canal → Carron Iron Works → Forth & Clyde Canal → PORT OF GRANGEMOUTH

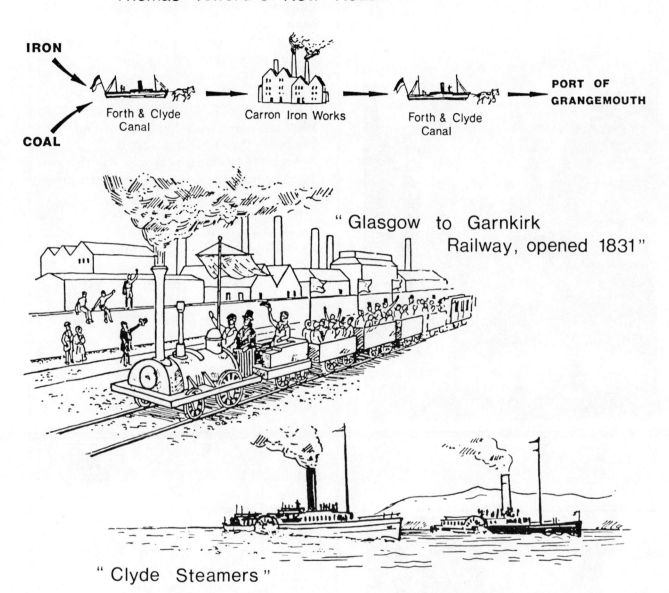

"Glasgow to Garnkirk Railway, opened 1831"

"Clyde Steamers"

Transport improved greatly between 1750 and 1900. You can find this out for yourself by filling in the blank spaces below. Use the pictures at the top of the page to help you.

At first, the roads were improved by men like ____. He used layers of ____. Also, his roads were on a slope so that the ____ drained away. New industries like the ____ Iron Works needed better transport. The ____ and ____ Canal was built to carry ____ and iron to these works. These materials were carried in barges pulled by ____. The same canal then carried the iron goods to the port of ____ to be sent to England or abroad.

Later, canals were replaced by railways. The railways were quicker and carried more goods. The first railway line was opened in the year ____. It ran from Glasgow to ____. It was built to carry coal to Glasgow. But the picture shows that it also carried ____.

Many other railway lines were opened all over Scotland. Even poor people could afford to travel by train. By 1900 many people from Glasgow were able to go on holiday down the Clyde coast either by train or ____.

Travel by Road

Around 1900 more and more people were using roads for travel. This was to change life in the streets of our towns.

Here are two pictures of streets in Glasgow in 1900 and 1914. We are going to use these pictures to help us find out how streets have changed between those days and today.

Things to do

1 Copy the following passage into your jotter filling in the blank spaces:

By 1914 only a very few rich people owned ____. Most people would travel by ____. They were powered by ____, and they ran on ____ on the road. Today they have been replaced by ____.

In 1900 heavy goods were carried through town streets by ____.

Today the same goods are carried by ____.

Even the road surface has changed. In 1900 the roads were made of cobbled ____. But today they have a surface of ____.

2 Even by 1914 there were still few vehicles on the town roads. As a result, cars could drive and park almost anywhere.

But today the roads are very busy. It is necessary to direct traffic to stop accidents. The easiest way of doing this is by using traffic signs. Here are a selection of traffic signs used today. Each sign has a letter.

(a) Which signs deal with each of these ways of directing traffic? Put the correct letters in the brackets.

No Parking ( ).

Junctions ( ), ( ), ( ).

Street directions ( ), ( ), ( ).

(b) Now colour in the traffic signs, using this colour code:

White −1 Blue −2

Red −3 Black −4

Roads

After 1900 good roads were built all over Scotland. Today every town and small village can be reached by road.

In recent years, it has been necessary to build much wider roads. This is because of the thousands of cars, buses and lorries that now use the roads. Also, vehicles are able to travel much faster than before. Today, Scotland has several motorways with two or three lanes in each direction.

Look at the road map below. You will now learn how to use a road map.

Things to do

1 What are the two reasons why roads are much wider today?
2 The **scale** of the map is ____ centimetre on the map for every ____ kilometres on the road.
3 The type or **class** of a road is shown by a letter:
   M – motorway; A – major road; B – minor road.
   Now find the number of these roads.
   (a) The three motorways on the map.
   (b) Road from Doune to Dunblane.
   (c) Road from Kippen to Fintry.
4 **Distances** between places are shown like this ▸ 8 ◂ = 8 kilometres.

What is the distance between:
(a) Callander and Doune.
(b) Greenloaning and Dunblane.
You can also measure distances by using a ruler and the scale. Work out the distance between:
(c) Comrie and Dunblane.
(d) Strathyre and Doune.
5 You are now going to **plan a route** by road. You are to go by car from Kilsyth to Callander.

Write down the route you would take. For each stage of the journey, you should mention the following: name of the place or town; number of road; direction to be taken; distance.
6 Now you are going to travel from Cumbernauld to Comrie. Trace your route from the map, then colour it in using these colours:
   motorway – blue
   A Road – green
   B Road – red
7 You will notice that there are very few roads around the letters NN and NS. Can you think of two reasons for this?
8 You live in Lennoxtown. You and your friend are going for a day trip by bicycle. You will have lunch at the side of the Lake of Menteith. Plan out a round trip which will take you back to Lennoxtown.

Work out how many kilometres you have cycled.

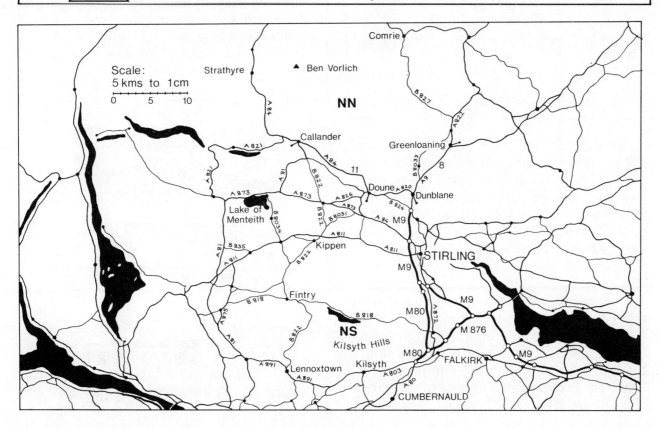

Railways

The first railways in Scotland were opened in the 1820s. From 1840 to 1940 railway lines were opened all over Scotland, and also between Scotland and England. The 1940s saw the first major change to our railways. In 1948 the railways were **nationalized**. The chart below shows what happened.

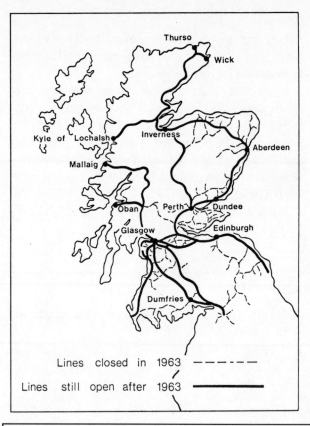

Lines closed in 1963 — — — —
Lines still open after 1963 ————

1945

RAILWAYS OWNED BY

7

PRIVATE COMPANIES

(NORTH BRITISH; HIGHLAND; GLASGOW AND SOUTH WESTERN; CALEDONIAN; WEST HIGHLAND RAILWAY COMPANIES)

NATIONALISATION

1948

RAILWAYS OWNED BY THE STATE AND CALLED BRITISH RAILWAYS (LATER BRITISH RAIL)

Things to do

1 Who owned the railways in 1945?
Who owned the railways in 1948?
Who cut the number of railway lines in 1963?
How many stations were closed?
People who lived in (town/country) areas were left without trains.

2 After 1963 the government tried to improve the railways.
Look at the pictures below and complete the sentence. The types of trains were changed from ____ to ____ and later ____

The next change came in 1963. The railways had been losing £87 million each year. Dr Beeching, who was asked by the government to make the railways profitable, said that about 66 per cent of railway lines had to close. Also, over 300 stations were to close. The map shows how much of Scotland's railway network was closed down, and what was left.

As a result of Beeching's cuts, only two types of rail links were left. Firstly, these are **long distance** trains between large towns like I____, D____, A____, and P____. Secondly, there are the short distance **commuter** services. They run to towns around the big cities of G____ and E____.

The railways also started to carry more heavy goods or freight. Rearrange the letters to find what items they carried: olac; rsac; mencte; rino; eelst; tlaect; clsheacmi.

Travel by train has changed over the years. Let us look at a journey from Inverness to Perth in 1905 and in 1985. It is a total of 190 kilometres.

Look carefully at the train and timetable for the different years.

1985

Inverness – Perth

Inverness	d. 14.30
Aviemore	d. 15.12
Kingussie	d. 15.24
Pitlochry	d. 16.12
Perth	d. 16.50
↓	
London	a. 23.31

1905

Inverness – Perth

Inverness	d. 11.05 a.m
Grantown	d. 12.15 p.m.
Aviemore	d. 12.43 p.m.
Kingussie	d. 1.10 p.m.
Struan	d. 1.42 p.m.
Pitlochry	d. 1.50 p.m.
Perth	a. 3.35 p.m.
↓	
London	a. 5.50 a.m.

Things to do

1 What is the main difference between the train of 1905 and that of 1985?

2 What fuel was needed for each of the trains?

3 What do the letters **d** and **a** stand for?

4 What difference do you notice between the type of clock used in 1905 and that used in 1985?

5 How long did it take to travel from Inverness to Perth in (a) 1905, (b) 1985?

6 How long did it take to go from Kingussie to Pitlochry in (a) 1905, (b) 1985?

7 How many stations did these fast trains stop at between Inverness and Perth in (a) 1905, (b) 1985?

8 Which stations did trains no longer stop at in 1985?

9 How long did it take to travel by train to London from Inverness in (a) 1905, (b) 1985?

Travel by Air – Class Project

Today many people travel by plane. It is the quickest way to go long distances. We are going to look at the history of air travel in six stages.

The class should be divided into six groups. Each group will work on one of the six stages of air travel.

Below there is a picture and short piece of information on each of the six stages. This is intended to give each group a background of information. To make up their part of the project, each group will need to get much more information from other books. This is called **research**.

Each group should make up their own part of the class project. This should include both pictures and writing. The six stages should then be put together to make up the class project on the history of air travel.

Early Attempts to Fly

In 1503 John Damian tried to fly from Stirling to France. He covered his whole body with feathers and took off from the castle walls. He fell into the mud at the foot of the walls and broke his leg. All other attempts like this also failed.

The First Flight

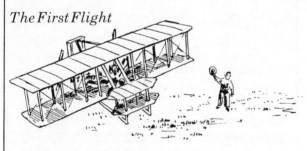

In 1903 the Wright brothers made the first flight in a plane. It lasted only 12 seconds. Longer flights soon followed.

The First World War (1914–1918)

Planes became bigger and faster during the war. They were an important new weapon. They were used to find out information about enemy soldiers and also to bomb enemy trenches. Famous pilots or 'aces' would fight each other in the skies. They were called 'dog-fights'.

People Travel by Plane

After the war old bombers were used to carry passengers. Planes were built to fly further. From 1919 people could fly regularly from London to Paris. People also flew in airships (large balloons filled with gas).

In 1927 Lindbergh was the first man to fly from America to Europe on his own. In 1930 Amy Johnson flew from London to Australia.

The Second World War (1939–1945)

Again war greatly improved planes. Large planes dropped hundreds of bombs on big cities. Small British fighter planes like the Spitfire and Hurricane won the Battle of Britain in 1940. By the end of the war jet planes had appeared. They could travel at 900 k.p.h.

Travel by plane today

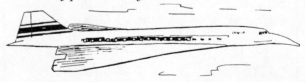

Today people can travel all over the world by plane. Millions of passengers use planes to travel for business and holidays. Concorde was built by Britain and France and can carry over 100 passengers to America in only four hours.

Unit 7

How We Are Governed

How are we governed today? It is very important that you know how our government works.

Britain today is a **democracy**. That means it is the **people** who decide who should rule the country.

Now let us find out how this democracy works? Fill in the missing words in the passage. Use the pictures at the bottom of the page to help you.

There must be an election every ____ years. At this people over ____ years of age can vote. In this way 630 members are elected to ____. They are called MPs and sit in the House of Commons. They are given the job of making new ____.

The ____ is the head of state. After the election she/he calls on the leader of the party with the most MPs to become ____ ____. This person now appoints 20 to 25 leading members of the winning party to form the ____. It is this group that makes the important decisions in the country.

Parliament

18

5

The Cabinet

How We Got the Vote

In 1830 only 10 per cent of men over the age of 21 had the right to vote. These men owned either a house or land. In 1832 the number of voters was increased by 5 per cent. The vote was given to farmers and shopkeepers.

About 40 per cent of men had the vote 35 years later. This now included many factory workers. In 1884 all men over the age of 21 were at last given the vote. Miners and farmworkers were the last to get the vote. But still no women could vote.

1900

1900 - 1914

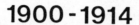

1914

1914 - 1918

VOTES
FOR
WOMEN
OVER
30

1918

VOTES
FOR
WOMEN
OVER
21

1928

By 1900 still no women had the vote. Some women began to fight for the vote. They were called **Suffragettes**.

The pictures above show how women got the vote.

An Election to Parliament

Your name is Peter Brown. You are standing for election to Parliament as a **Labour candidate**. There are three other candidates. There are four days to go to the election. How are you going to get the votes of the people?

Here is a list of ways:

Meeting people in the town shopping centre.

Television interview.

Speech to local factory workers.

Driving round the streets in a car with a loud speaker.

Delivering leaflets to every door.

Evening speech in the town hall.

Interview with local newspaper.

Make up a diary of what you are going to do in these four days. You could divide each day into morning, afternoon and evening.

Now draw an election poster. You should put in your name, the name of your party and a short slogan.

The voting goes on all day. After the polling station closes, all the votes are counted.

Here is the result of the vote:

Brown, Peter   23 151
Smith, James   12 263
Jones, Susan   2 560
Lang, Jean   16 211

Has Peter Brown won? How do you know? The winner of the election now becomes a Member of Parliament for that area or **constituency**.

It is the day of the election. Throughout the day people go to their local **polling station** to vote. Look at the three pictures which show you how people vote.

Describe in your own words what is happening in each picture.

The Result of a General Election

There must be a general election every five years. This is to elect a new government. Look at the chart below. It gives the results of the election at the Dunfermline constituency.

Candidate	Votes
R.G. Douglas (Labour)	12 998
P. Davidson (Conservative)	10 524
F. Moyes (SDP/Alliance)	9 438
J. Fairlie (Scottish Nationalist)	2 798
S. Dobson (Ecology)	321

Total number of voters =   65 530
Labour majority in 1979 =   7 313

Things to do

1 How many candidates were there?
2 Who was elected as the MP?
3 What party did he stand for?
4 By how many votes did he beat the next candidate? This is called his **majority**.
5 By how many votes was the winner's majority up or down from the 1979 election?
6 Who was the Scottish Nationalist candidate? How many people voted for him?
7 What was the total number of people who voted?
8 How many people did not vote?

Now have a look at the results of the 1983 election for both Scotland and the whole United Kingdom. Opposite there are two **pie charts**. They show the percentage share of seats won by each of the four main parties. Colour them in, using the following colour code:

Conservative – blue
Labour   – red
Alliance   – yellow
Other parties – green

What differences do you notice between the results in Scotland and those in the whole of the United Kingdom?

1983 General Election: Number of Seats

Party	UK	Scotland
Conservative	397 (61%)	21 (29%)
Labour	209 (32%)	41 (57%)
Alliance	23 (4%)	8 (11%)
Other parties e.g. Scottish Nats.	21 (3%)	2 (3%)
Total	650	72

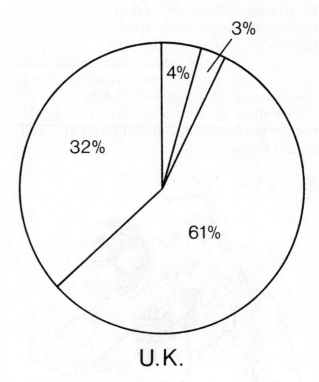

U.K.

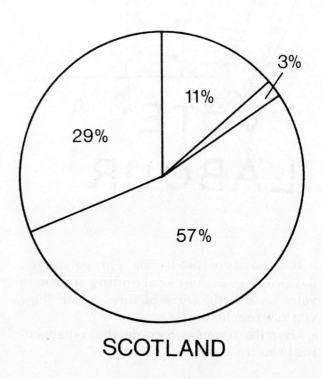

SCOTLAND

Should Scotland be Independent?

In 1707 Scotland and England joined into one united country.

Since 1707 both countries have ruled from London. In 1885 a special Government department was set up to look after Scottish affairs. In 1926 the Secretary of State for Scotland was given a place in the Cabinet for the first time. He looks after many aspects of Scottish affairs: the land, fishing, schools, health, houses, industry and the law.

Until the 1960s most people in Scotland voted for the labour, Conservative or Liberal Parties. But another party appeared in Scotland.

The **Scottish National Party** (SNP) was first formed in 1934. It had its first member of Parliament in 1945. It became more popular in the 1960s.

The SNP wants Scotland to be free and independent again, as it was before 1707. By 1974 it had 11 MPs in Parliament. Since then it has lost support. In the 1983 election the SNP won only two seats.

The Debate

The class should be organized for a debate. The question for debate is: 'Should Scotland be a separate country?' One pupil should be asked to speak *in favour* of the question. Here are some points to help him/her:

Scotland should own her own oil.

A lot of factories and shipyards have closed recently.

The Government in London does not seem interested in Scotland.

Not enough money is given to Scotland to build new hospitals, factories and schools.

Another pupil should speak *against* the question. Here are some points to help him/her:

Scotland and England have been joined for nearly 300 years.

Since 1707 both countries have become very rich.

We have the same language, money and army.

It would be silly to have customs posts at the border.

After both pupils have spoken, the rest of the class should say what they think. All pupils should then vote.

The Survey

Each pupil should make up a survey sheet. They should ask 10 people the question discussed in the class debate. For each person, your survey sheet should have three columns under the headings of *Yes*, *No*, and *Don't know*.

Many people believe that Scotland should have a greater say in her own affairs. As a result, in 1975 the Labour Government tried to give Scotland her own **Assembly** or Parliament. This was called **Devolution**. The government wanted to know if people in Scotland really wanted their own Assembly. As a result, a vote or **referendum** was held on 1 March 1979. But, it was also decided that at least 40 per cent must vote *yes* if the Assembly was to be granted. Here is how the vote went:

Yes – 32.8%
No – 30.8%

As a result, the plan for a Scottish Assembly failed.

Things to do

1 Write down in a sentence what each of these words mean: Devolution; Assembly; referendum.
2 Explain why the plan for an Assembly failed?
3 How many people did not vote at all?

Local Government

For the last 500 years local government in Scotland has been based on the **counties**. Here are some examples: Ayrshire, Banffshire, Renfrewshire.

In 1973 local government was changed. The old counties were replaced by **Regions** and **Districts**. Also, each local area was given its own **community council**. Here is a map of the **Regions of Scotland**.

Things to do

1 Copy and complete the blanks by writing in the full name of the Regions and their headquarters. Populations are given in brackets.

Region	Headquarters
H_____ (175 000)	I_____
G_____ (453 000)	A_____
T_____ (402 000)	D_____

Region	Headquarters
C_____ (270 000)	S_____
F_____ (338 000)	C_____
L_____ (755 000)	E_____
S_____ (2 488 000)	G_____
D_____&G_____ (143 000)	D_____
B_____ (100 000)	St.B_____

2 How many Regions are there on the mainland of Scotland?

3 There are also three Island Authorities (population 66 000). What are their names?

4 Name the Region with the following:
   (a) largest area of land.
   (b) smallest area of land.
   (c) largest number of people.
   (d) smallest number of people.

5 Now work out the total population of Scotland.

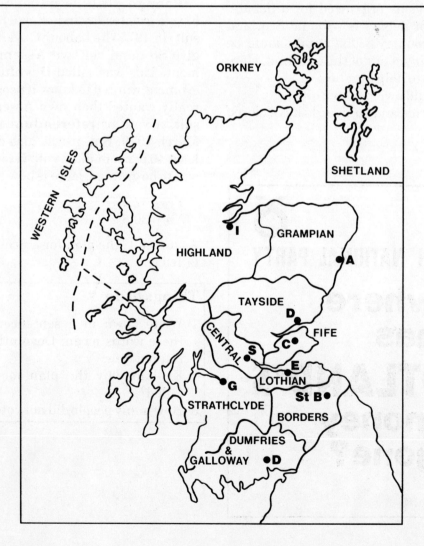

Here is a map of the **Districts** within Grampian Region. How many Districts are there?

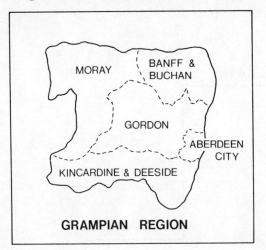

GRAMPIAN REGION

The Regions and Districts look after different local services. The small pictures below show many of these services.

Things to do

1 Make a list of the services provided by the Region and another of services provided by the District.
2 Which local authority would you go to if you wanted:
   (a) to get rubbish lifted?
   (b) to book a football pitch?
   (c) to repair a burst water pipe?
   (d) to repair a hole in the road?
   (e) to arrange for a burial?
   (f) to pay your council house rent?

Services Provided by the Region

Services Provided by the District

The **Community Council** deals with local needs. The picture below shows the sort of thing it can become involved in. Describe in your own words what is going on.

Where does local government get its money from? The chart below tells you how Strathclyde Region gets its money.

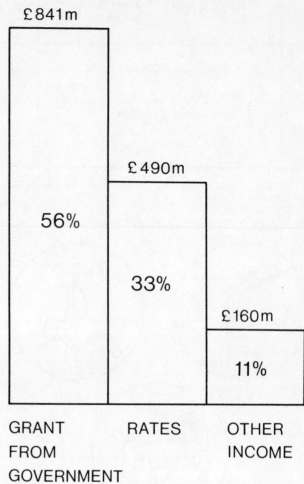

£841m

£490m

56%

33%

£160m

11%

GRANT
FROM
GOVERNMENT

RATES

OTHER
INCOME

Things to do

1 Where does most of the money come from?
2 What is the total amount of money that the Region has to spend?
3 Most of the 'Other Income' taken in by the Region is in charges for some of the services. Can you think of a service that people have to pay for?
4 Rates are paid by people who own their houses. How much each person pays is based on the **rateable value** of the house. This is how it is worked out: Rateable value of the house = £150. The rate is set at 80p in the £. The owner of the house pays: £____ × ____p = £120 to the Region.